★ JIMMY ★
THE BARTENDER'S
Guide to Life

Advice on
Women • Sex • Money • Work
and Other Stuff That Screws Up Men's Lives

by **James "Jimmy the Bartender" Kennedy**
with Denis Boyles

Rodale Press, Inc.
Emmaus, Pennsylvania

Notice

The advice in this book is presented to entertain, to serve as an aid to busy bartenders, and to provide legitimate guidance about relationships and common life situations. But please—if you are facing difficult decisions about your health, marriage, friendships, or job, don't rely on advice from a bartender. Seek competent professional help.

Cover and Interior Designer: Christopher Rhoads
Cover Photographer: Andrew Kist
Illustrator: Jason Schneider

Library of Congress Cataloging-in-Publication Data

Kennedy, James (James Ignatius Meloy)
    Jimmy the Bartender's guide to life / by James "Jimmy the Bartender" Kennedy ; with Denis Boyles.
        p.   cm.
    ISBN 1–57954–172–0 paperback
    1. Men—Conduct of life.   I. Boyles, Denis.   II. Title.
BJ1601K46   1999
646.7—dc21   99–33828

Distributed to the book trade by St. Martin's Press

2   4   6   8   10   9   7   5   3   1   paperback

Visit us on the Web at www.menshealthbooks.com, or call us toll-free at (800) 848-4735.

OUR PURPOSE

We inspire and enable people to improve their lives and the world around them.

CONTENTS

INTRODUCTION

INTRODUCTION

Jimmy's always doing the talking. But for once, I'm going to talk for both of us.

Jimmy's a shy but popular guy, and it's not hard to see why. The spirit of Jimmy the Bartender is everywhere spirits are served—in small, cozy, neighborhood taverns and big-deal, downtown, fancy-schmancy saloons. Bartenders know that as different as some of these places are from each other, they all have one thing in common: guys with problems. And not just drinking problems, either.

I have this theory about why guys ask bartenders for advice. I think it's because when you're in a bar having a few drinks, you don't realize you're getting dumber and dumber by the shot. Meanwhile, the longer you drink, the smarter the guy behind the bar gets—assuming he isn't drinking on the job. When a guy's so stupid that he's almost falling over, who's he going to ask for advice? Right. The smartest man he can find.

Like Jimmy, I've spent my fair share of time in saloons on both sides of the bar. I'm not jaded and I'm not cynical. But I am, I guess, what you'd call "experienced." I hear the same questions asked over and over again, and sometimes by the same kinds of guys. For example, for all you real bartenders out there, here is a barkeep's list of the 10 most-frequently used answers. You drinkers can figure out the questions on your own:

1. In the back, past the kitchen, first door on the right.

2. Eventually, she'll find out.

3. It's for you—and, believe me, she knows you're here.

4. Yes, that's exactly what you said.

5. No. Your boss won't give you a raise unless you ask him.

6. Do what you want, but she'll look worse in the morning. And so will you.

7. When women say "friends"—as in, "Let's just be friends"—they mean "strangers."

8. No, you shouldn't. Call a cab. It's cheaper than calling a lawyer.

9. Honey, if you want to marry him, don't start your honeymoon in here.

10. Ask her yourself.

I'm not putting anybody down here. I mean, as the guy on the civilian side of a bar, I'm just as likely to ask the same questions as anybody else. But the fact that this list of answers covers maybe 90 percent of all the questions a bartender gets might say something about human nature, not to mention the leveling effects of alcohol.

For the most part, a guy asking a bartender a question just wants to hear somebody tell him that what he *thought* was the right thing really *is* the right thing. That's how little confidence any of us has in our own common sense anymore.

But every now and then, you see a guy who really just doesn't have a clue, even when the evidence is right in front of him. Men really do ask a bartender if their wives are cheating on them. They really do ask if their boss thinks they're worthless or if their kids are going to jail. Life sometimes just gets so confusing that all you can do is put your head in a fog and ask somebody else to navigate.

Maybe it's a sign of the times. My old man used to say that if you ever went to a town and saw more churches than bars, something was wrong. His theory was that it was a supply-and-demand thing. You needed a ready supply of sinners if you wanted to put a value on virtue. But today, there's so much value placed on sin—and I mean on all kinds of misbehavior, whether it's being an absentee parent so you can get rich or putting your marriage on ice so you can get laid—that virtue seems kind of irrelevant. Until, that is, you need a little of it. Even the worst of us finds out sooner or later that being bad doesn't make us feel good. There's always a hangover in the morning.

Anyway, I hope you enjoy Jimmy's little book here. Jim wants to thank Ron Geraci, the guy who edits his section of *Men's Health*, from the bottom of his mug. If more guys were like him, more women would be happy, more children would be fed, the world would be a better place, and more bartenders would be working at real jobs. And if you think *he's* smart, you should meet Mike, the guy who hired him.

We also want to thank all the Joes out there who write in. We all have problems, and we're no better than anybody else. As Jimmy might put it, "I'm just lucky to be the guy doing the pouring."

Here's looking at you.

Denis Boyles
James Ignatius Meloy Kennedy

. . . but if you call him anything other than Jimmy, he'll bounce you *right now*.

Alcohol,
as a Dietary Supplement

Chemically, we're talking about poisons here.

Dear Jimmy,
  I just bought myself a home gym set and formulated a workout schedule, and I'm eating healthier. My question to you is about alcohol. I am not an alcoholic but I do enjoy having a few drinks at night when in the mood. Which alcoholic drinks have the most to least calories (beer, whiskey, wine), and how often should or could I have a drink at night? And if so, what type of drink? Or should I only drink on the weekends? Or if I drink at all, will it cause me to not get abs of steel?

—Adam, New Brunswick, N.J.

While I can honestly tell you that a drinking habit will one day give your funeral guests more interesting stories, it just won't help your physique much, unless you're going for the gut and not for the glory. Sorry. But what did you expect me to say? Look, all alcoholic drinks have plenty of calories. A bottle of good-quality dark beer can be 300 calories. That's like liquid french fries. Even a glass of dry wine is upwards of 90 calories. Get it? You can chug a day's worth of chow in half an hour. Plus, tipsy people eat like pigs. That's why we clear about a million a week on mozzarella sticks. You want a good low-cal mixed drink? Order a scotch and soda, but hold the scotch. Sorry, no magic bullets here. Alcohol will make you fat.

  Or, you can have a drink or two each night, as long as you're willing to sweat off an extra 1,000 calories each week to pay for it. Just drinking on the weekends annoys professional barkeeps like me, 'cause you guys tend to cram it all in on Saturday night and end up messing the bathroom floor.

Ambition,
Thwarted

Ambition isn't just blind, but deaf and dumb, too.

Dear Jimmy,
   I just can't seem to get ahead at work. I work my ass off every day, 12 hours a day, 7 days a week. My supervisors are totally happy with me, but they just don't understand how important it is to me to move up and be given more responsibility. I've told them, but they don't seem to hear me. What do I do?

—Lee, Erie, Pa.

I've seen blind ambition a million times. Guy comes in, makes eyes at a girl. She's gorgeous. He isn't. But he's ambitious. So he does everything he can to get her attention. She may smile, she may nod, but really, it's like he's invisible. And because he's trying so hard, he's blind. He can do tricks for her for the rest of his life, but it won't matter. Why? Because in her own way, she's already told him he's a loser, and no matter what else he does after that, he's going nowhere with her. What advice would you give the guy? You'd tell him to walk, right?

Well, it's the same for you. Your boss is the good-looking babe in my bar. You're the guy making all the effort to be charming and cool. You've made it clear that the reason you're working so hard is that you want to get ahead. Now it's time to see if you're going to get lucky. When the next slot above you opens up, go to your supervisor and ask for the job. If he says no, walk, because no matter how hard you're working, he's telling you that he sees you as a loser, and nothing will ever change that. The good news is, you'll know. So you may still be ambitious. But at least you won't be blind.

After-Effects,
of Drinking

It ain't over until the fat man swings.

Dear Jimmy,
  When I go out drinking, I get the worst hangovers if I have only a few drinks. But I feel perfectly fine the next morning when I have a lot of drinks. With my buddies, it's the exact opposite. Is something wrong here, or am I just destined for a liver transplant?

—Randy, Salinas, Calif.

It's chemistry. I used to have a doc who drank in my bar. This guy had more theories than Oliver Stone. One of his ideas was that the alcohol from a few drinks wrecks your sleep, so you wake up miserably tired—sort of like you hadn't gone to bed at all. But the alcohol from lots of drinks wrecks your sleep even worse—and, especially if you're a beer-drinker, since you also load your body full of sweet carbohydrates and tons of sugary calories. This makes you wake up feeling not only like you hadn't gone to bed but also like you had eaten five chocolate bars during a sleepless night. The hangover hell should kick in by noon, though. If it doesn't, it means you're very young and it will kick in someday soon. Just ask any guy with an enormous beer gut. You sound too smart to ever get to the new-liver stage. On the other hand, I have noticed that customers who stop caring about hangovers usually disappear for one reason or another.

Apologies,
the Art of Making

Being President means you never have to say, "I'm sorry." Attention, everybody else: You're forgiven.

Dear Jimmy,

Several weekends ago, I got really hammered and said something really rude to a woman friend's substantially older boyfriend. This comment did a lot of damage. Any suggestions on how to repair this mistake?

—John, Yakima, Wash.

One little comment can do a lot of damage. I once worked with a guy for 5 years. We got to be real friends. One night, he accused me of taking a tip—a lousy two-buck tip. I think it was a deuce, but to tell you the truth, I don't even remember. What I remember is that the guy never apologized, and so to this day, I think he's a jerk. When somebody's father dies, or when you've done something so stupid you wish *you* could die, there's only one thing you can say: "I'm sorry." Nothing fancy, nothing complicated. Don't say it until you mean it, then say it like you do. After that, it's their problem.

Backs,
Doing Stuff Behind

If a guy cheats in the woods but nobody hears him, does it count?

Dear Jimmy,

I'm 40. I spend a lot of time at work with a 24-year-old woman friend. This makes my wife crazy. She seems to think that my co-worker would bed me in a second if she had the chance. So my wife asked me not to spend as much time with her. But here's the problem: I still talk to this girl. I tell her not to mention anything to my wife (whom she knows). I really do enjoy talking to her and spending time with her. But I also realize I am happily married and I don't want anything else to come of it. Anyway, the question is, is this wrong?

—Dave, Springfield, Ill.

Sure. Of course it's wrong. It's wrong of your wife to make that kind of request, but what the hey, you're married to her, and part of the deal with that is you have to do what you can to make her comfortable. If she were doing the same thing with some guy, you'd probably do the same thing, just because it makes you feel rotten. You'd be wrong, too. But you'd expect her to go along with it because you know that married people should be nice to each other like that.

So she's wrong on that count. But you? You're wrong on four counts. First, guilty of not giving your wife a break. Second, guilty of lying to her and doing stuff behind her back. Third, guilty of humiliating her by asking another woman, one she knows, to keep the chats to herself. Fourth, guilty of putting the co-worker in the position of being a liar, too.

Bait and Switch,
the Real Cost of

If you cheat your customers, you cheat yourself.

Dear Jimmy,

Whenever I go somewhere with my buddy and he sees a girl he likes, he makes me get her phone number. He doesn't understand that a chick would respect him more if he had the balls to do it himself. I don't know how to get him to do this stuff himself. What do you say?

—Eddie, Rochester, N.Y.

We got Abbot and Costello here. What, does he slap you around and stick you with the beer tab, too? A guy came up to the bar one night, and he holds up a half-empty beer and says, "This Foster's is flat. Can I trade it for a Guinness?" I could see his friend watching us from a table in the barroom. I knew two things: I had just dragged in a new Foster's keg that afternoon, and this fellow in front of me only drinks light beer. I began filling a Guinness and said, "No problem, buddy. Are you gonna take a piss for your pal later, too?" He managed to laugh, but he got the point. If you don't have the cojones to risk making a jackass out of yourself by asking an awkward question, you don't deserve to get whatever it is you want.

See, Ed, your friend doesn't think that you're any better at getting a gal's number than he is—he just thinks you should be the one who looks like a jackass if she says no. Tell him that any number you get from now on, you're keeping. Then, keep the next one and take the girl out instead of wasting your time with him.

Beer,
Glasses for

There shouldn't be anything esoteric about beer. But somebody's always gotta screw things up.

Dear Jimmy,
A friend of mine tried to tell me that there were different kinds of glasses for different beers. The guy is a snob, so I didn't believe him. I even asked my local bartender, and he said he didn't know—all he used were mugs. The guy insists. Is he right?

—Chet, El Paso, Tex.

I hate to admit it, but he is. Here's the glass list.

Tumbler. The standard widemouthed glass. Use it for lagers.

Snifter. Kind of a narrower version of the brandy glass. Use it for dark ales and barley wines.

Tulip. Shaped like the flower, stupid, with a drinking lip that tapers out. Should hold a whole bottle of golden ale.

Flute. Tall and thin, sitting on a stem. Fruity, boutique brews.

Chalice. What a Viking would drink from—a big, deep goblet. Stouts and porters.

Stein. A big mug. All the above.

I'm also one bartender who approves of by-the-neck drinkers of conventional bottled brews. Now drink up.

Best Friends,
Who Despise Wives

Here are two questions about best friends and wives.
Bartenders call that a "bad mix"—here's why.

Dear Jimmy,

My wife and my best friend don't get along, to put it mildly. And, of course, I'm caught in the middle. "Tom" has been rude to her since the day they met, and while she didn't object, I know she wasn't happy about him being my best man. I can't say I blame her, but that's always been his style. He's a harsh guy and she can be a little sensitive at times. I know it makes no sense, but he's my best friend and he's always been there for me. But then, she's my wife, and things he says and does hurt her. I'm at my wit's end; he and I have talked, yelled, and almost come to blows over this. Still, nothing gets any better. HELP!

—Raphael, San Diego

Caught in the middle? Hate to break it to you, pally, but you're not in the middle. You're sidelined. Your "best friend" is rude to your wife, ignores what you say to him, puts stress on your marriage, and you want help from me? Okay, here: Walk up to your buddy with this book. Put your finger on the next paragraph and read it out loud.

"You're rude to my wife. You have no respect for my marriage. You won't listen to me when I tell you to knock it off. So listen to this: Get lost. Never speak to me again until you can treat my wife with the dignity she deserves. See ya."

Okay? Hey—you there? Didn't faint, did you? Now, walk away. When you get home, give your new best friend a kiss.

Best Friends,
Wives Who Despise

Sometimes, a man's wife is his best friend. But then, there are always dogs.

Dear Jimmy,

My friend of 20 years was just married, and his new wife hates me. Reason: I'm still single, so she says I'm a crappy influence on him. I'm not a bad influence on anybody, Jim. Now the guy lies about meeting me so he can keep peace with his wife. I'm pretty peeved. What should I do?

—Art, Oswego, N.Y.

This one is a classic. Here we have a babe who's so worried about her own shortcomings that she needs to grab her husband by the cojones and squeeze the joy right out of his life. Almost overnight, he becomes the type of passive coward that used to give both of you a good laugh. Makes me sick, Art.

Here's what you do: Make her worst nightmare come true. She's afraid you'll tell the guy the truth—that she's a control freak who's ruining him. So tell him. Tell him he's a wimp and you're ashamed of him. And tell him it's only a matter of time before she starts hating him for being a spineless nonman, a worthless pile of Barcalounger ballast. She'll whine to all her friends, then she'll whine to her boyfriend—while I'm mixing sea breezes for both of them. Get the point?

So tell your buddy to grow a backbone right now, or he'll be facing a decade of overfed misery. He'll be furious with you for coming down so hard, of course. Probably won't talk to you for years. But who cares? If you keep quiet, he'll just turn into a pathetic weasel who ignores you anyhow. And he'll eventually knock on your door with a duffel after she lets the boyfriend move in. The "I told you so" won't be worth it, Art.

Best Man,
Duties of a

Be a prop, not the whole show.

Dear Jimmy,
  I am going to be the best man at a wedding. I know what to do in the ceremony, how to handle the ring, all that. But I want to do the speech right. Who should I address? Should I throw something in for a laugh? Should it all be serious? How long should it be? How do I start it? How should I end it? Some advice would be greatly appreciated.

Noel, El Paso, Tex.

I don't want you to make this too complicated, Noel, so I won't make it complicated either. Here's how I'd want it done if you were doing this at my own son's wedding: Give a salute to the groom, but address the room. Give the groom's story. Repeat what he said about his bride to you when they first met. Mention the weird thing he did that let all his pals know he was over the edge for her. Talk about how she's made him a better man. Give your own thoughts of why the marriage is perfect and will last forever. Details. Use details. Keep it light. Keep it totally clean. And talk like you're speaking to me— at ease. Three, maybe 4 minutes, that's it. Remember this: You don't want to be the memory they all have of this day. You're strictly a supporting actor, so please don't eat the scenery.

Blindness,
of Friends, Regarding Their Wives

Sometimes, all you can do is help them across the street.

Dear Jimmy,
My good friend's wife is sleeping all over town. I've seen her run her game, and it bothers me that he doesn't believe me when I say she's bad news. He looks like a total moron while his wife is out there skanking up the place. What would it take to get it through his head that he's married to a prostitute?

—Miles, Chicago

What would it take? Well, how about a receipt?

Look, he knows who he's married to and you've done your bit by telling him. Now stay out of it, or your buddy will lose his best friend *and* his wife. Nobody wants to be told something he already knows. So assume he's into it and that he's dealing with it his own way, which is none of your business. Or assume he's not, but that he doesn't want you to get into it with him.

Bloody Mary,
the Perfect Mix

I put three classic drink recipes in this book. This is one.

Dear Jimmy,

How do I make a Bloody Mary? I keep getting these different recipes and none of them work out right. I even tried one where I put tomatoes in a blender, but it just tasted like a watered-down drink. How does a pro do it?

—Kevin, San Francisco

As my wife will tell you, there are lots of things I can do in my sleep. This is one. Now the place I'm working uses the premixed stuff. But here's how I'd do it if I had company coming.

Get a big pitcher and mix a 24-ounce can of tomato juice, the juice from a decent-size lemon, a little more than a teaspoon of Worcestershire sauce, a little less than a teaspoon of Tabasco, some salt—like maybe a third of a teaspoon—about the same amount of pepper, and—trust me, this is important—about a half a teaspoon of freshly ground horseradish root. You can get it at the store. Peel off the outer layer of the root and grate it with one of those cheese graters. Now you've got the mix.

Line up a bunch of glasses and run a lemon wedge around the rim of each of them. Turn them upside down in a bowl with salt in it. Believe it or not, I like table salt, but a lot of guys prefer margarita-style salt, which is a little more coarse. Put ice in the glass and a celery stalk (or a slice of lemon or whatever you feel like, short of little umbrellas). If you use a pourer on your vodka bottle, give it a three-count pour; otherwise, put in a healthy shot. Now add the mix. If you want to be fruity, add a tiny flake or two of parsley. If you can do this fast, women will admire you. Drunks will love you.

Jimmy's List

The Five Requirements of a Date

If it doesn't have all of these, you're just hanging out.

1. MAKE IT CLEAR IT'S A DATE. If you make it seem like it's not a big deal, then that's how it'll turn out.

2. MAKE A PLAN. Give your date a beginning, a middle, and an end—just like a sitcom.

3. DRESS FOR THE OCCASION. Whatever the occasion is.

4. KEEP YOUR PROBLEMS TO YOURSELF. No griping about work, old girlfriends, or family ills.

5. PICK UP THE TAB. Including mine.

Here's a tip: At the end, when you walk her to her door? Kiss her. On the mouth. But keep it closed, for pity's sake.

Body Jewelry,
Secrets of

If you've already got a hole in your head, you might as well fill it up with something nice.

Dear Jimmy,
  Which is the politically correct ear to pierce nowadays?

—Oliver, New York City

A woman's.

Hey, Ollie, maybe it's because my grandfather's name was Oliver, and I can't see him ever playing fashion pirate with a pierced ear. Or maybe I'm just too old. But I've been through the long-hair thing and the Mohawk thing and the tattoo thing and now the facial hardware thing. I think there should be a law saying that you can't make a permanent idiot out of yourself until you're over 40. Forty-year-old guys wearing ponytails and earrings—they know they look stupid. But at 40 or 50, you don't have to care anymore. If you're younger than that, you're doing this stuff to look cool. If you have to work that hard to appear to be cool, you can't be cool, period. I have seen five zillion guys walk into a bar trying to look cool to everybody else. But the guys who look coolest are the guys who don't try to look cool at all. They just are.

Boom,
How to Lower the

The difference between fireworks and firearms is in the aim and the intent.

Dear Jimmy,
I had an affair with a married gal, but I cut it off after 10 years of just boom, boom, boom. I got sick and tired of it. But this gal got it going again when she came to my home one night and I forgot to lock my door. As I was asleep, she came in, and you know the rest. Boom, boom, boom. Sex is great, but this has to stop, especially since I've met another gal. I like her a lot, and we're good friends, but she works so much that she has little time for me boom-wise, which brings me back to the married gal. How can I get out of this mess before I drive myself crazy? I need sex, but not from someone who I feel just uses me for that.

—Thompson, Pueblo, Colo.

Who's using who here? When her husband drives his Ranchero through your front door one night, that should make the decision easier for you. You stop bucking married women and using other people for sex the same way you stop smoking, robbing old people, or kicking dogs. You just stop. How? Look at your new squeeze for inspiration: Keep busy. Try building a life from scratch. That ought to do it. Meanwhile, keep your door locked at night.

The Boss,
Asking Out

If Jack Kevorkian were a career counselor, Bruce would be his first client.

Dear Jimmy,

I recently started working a great job, probably the best I've ever had so far. There doesn't seem to be much wrong with this job, but there is one problem. One of my managers is hot, and I mean hot. She interviewed me, and during the interview, I thought I detected a little flirting going on, but I'm not sure. Now, around the work place, she smiles at me and always goes out of her way to talk to me. The problem is she's my boss, but she seems to be initiating some flirting. Is it okay to ask her out?

—Bruce, Milwaukee

Tell you what, Bruce. When you wake up in your own bed and your boss is next to you stark naked, then you can figure it's safe to ask her out. But not until. If this woman is smart enough to be living alone and if she is genuinely attracted to you, then all you have to do is smile and wait. Why? Because she'll ask you out. And the reason she'll do that is she's smart enough to know that you can't possibly ask her out. If she can't figure that out, you don't want to know her anyway.

Brawl,
How to Stop a Barroom

You're the captain, captain.

Dear Jimmy,
  I'm a fellow bartender. The other night, a fight started in my bar and it was an unholy mess. I broke it up, but I guess I handled it wrong. I'm not sure what I should have done differently. What do you do?

—Stu, Kansas City, Mo.

The big trick isn't the bat I keep behind the bar, and it isn't how loud I can shout. The whole secret to keeping a bar fight from turning into a brawl is to move fast and get in the middle. Don't pay any attention to anything anybody's saying, because it doesn't matter. Just break them up fast. If the confrontation has gone on for more than 10 seconds, you've lost it. That seems like a short amount of time, but you know how it is: You can see a fight coming a mile away. Drunk guys looking for a fight in a bar just can't keep a secret. So jump quick and just keep saying, "Out you go, both of you," until they're gone.

Breaking Up,
Periods of Craziness Following

All seven ages of a man rolled into one nutty year.

Dear Jimmy,

I was engaged to a girl for 3 years. Then one day without any real explanation, she broke up with me. I spoke with her just last week only to find out that she is now dating someone new. It's only been 60 days since we stopped seeing one another. I'll admit I am a sap for this girl, but what is the typical mourning period following a breakup, and am I being an idiot to think that she didn't break up with me for this guy? Any advice on dealing with this situation would be helpful. We are in our early thirties.

—Doug, Columbus, Ohio

Okay, here it is, my original heartbreak schedule. I'm not guessing at this, either; I've been through it so many times that I wrote this down, took it to Kinko's, and had them run off a bunch of copies so that when guys like you come in, I don't have to start from scratch.

If you break up with her:	If she breaks up with you:
Disbelief: 1 hour	**Disbelief:** 3 weeks
Anger: 2 minutes	**Anger:** 2 months
Regret: 1 week	**Regret:** 3 months
Weird obsession: 15 minutes	**Weird obsession:** 6 months
Regaining composure: 1 day	**Regaining composure:** 2 years
Revenge dating: 1 month	**Revenge dating:** 1 year
Back to normal: 6 weeks	**Back to normal:** Dream on

These are worst-case scenarios, the end of the love-of-a-lifetime type of thing. For more casual break-ups, the whole healing process should be three weeks, unless you see her with another guy, in which case you should add a year. If the breakup is a divorce, multiply everything times two, add alimony and a dash of bitters.

Bridges,
Burning

One man's bridge is another man's business.

Dear Jimmy,
  I've been with my current company for 2 years now. I'm being groomed to assume the top position in my office, but I've been offered an opportunity that pays more money and gives me more responsibility. I want to take it, but my absence will put my manager in a real bind. If things don't work out, I'll never be able to return because my manager holds grudges against people that leave the company. I don't want to leave my manager high and dry, but this move will be good for me and my family. How can I explain this gracefully?

—Placido, Thousand Oaks, Calif.

You and your boss are talking two different languages here, so if you're thinking that eloquence will bail you out, you're wrong. The facts are these: Your company expects you to be loyal to them. Your family expects that you'll do what's right by them. The only way to bridge this gap is by making sure everybody's speaking the same language. So make sure you have the other job first, then go to your boss and spill the beans. He'll do one of two things. He'll either meet and beat the other offer or he'll say so long. I'm betting on number two. And that's fine, since I can't see owing any loyalty to a guy who's petty enough to hold grudges. If he's that kind of guy, believe me, you're giving him more than he deserves already. If there's a bridge to burn, torch that one. The other one leads to your future.

Brothers,
Long-Lost

Ever look for something for years, then find it right in front of you?

Dear Jimmy,
 I have a little brother (he's 32, I'm 39), and I used to beat him up when we were young. I'd like to be closer with him, but I can't seem to get around the fact that I bullied him. Any suggestions?

—Paul, Minneapolis

I have four brothers and I beat up every one of them unless they were busy beating me up. We're scattered all over the country, but we're tight because we know the others are there for us.

If you want to get closer to your brother, just get back into his life. Call him up. Shoot the breeze. Commiserate. Once you're a part of his life again, and once you let him be a part of yours again, the work's done, since there's nothing else you can be for each other but brothers.

And take it from a guy who got it and gave it: As bad as you feel about beating him up, he feels worse that you're beating yourself up now and keeping your distance.

Careers,
Hiding behind

All fathers have two jobs. Why do they pay all their attention to the easiest one?

Dear Jimmy,
I'm a 29-year-old software developer. I work some seriously long hours, including many weekends. But I have been promoted twice and doubled my salary in the past year. My wife isn't happy; she wants me to spend more time with her and our daughter. How do I strike a balance between work time and family time when my career is really starting to take off?

—Frank, Bryn Mawr, Pa.

Hey, Frank. What are you going to do with the money? Here's the bartender's equivalent. I see this every night. A guy gets to drinking with a couple of other guys. Pretty soon, they're tipsy, right on the edge of pure stupid. One guy gets a great idea and says to me, "Hey, Jim. Another round." I look at him and say, "Why? What are you going to do with it?" I tell them, stop now and have a cola or something, and you can go home happy. One more, and you get to put your head in my toilet.

So, you. What are you going to do with the money? Buy your kid a new childhood? Take the old lady out and marry her again? A man doesn't need talent or skill to make lots of money if he's willing to put in long hours and work hard. A drone can do that. The real genius is making lots of money by working less. Your career isn't taking off. You're carrying way too much baggage to get it off the ground. Lighten up and soar.

Celebrities,
the Appeal of

This time, what you see is not what you get.

Dear Jimmy,

I would very much like to meet the young and very attractive lady who anchors our local weekend news. How do I do this without her, or anyone else, for that matter, thinking that I'm some mental-case stalker? Which I'm not, by the way, just so you know. Any and all information would be gratefully appreciated. Thank you.

—Greg, Stroudsburg, Pa.

Turn off the TV. You might as well fall in love with somebody over the Internet. The principle is the same. You are attracted to somebody because of what you want her to be, not because of what she really is.

I remember this one place I worked. I wasn't there long, maybe a year. Busy place. Too busy. But all through that year, there was this guy—I called him the Mook—who could talk about nothing but this woman who would come into the place maybe once a week. You never knew when. She'd just show up with some friends, have a drink or two, then leave. So this guy would be there every night and sit at the end of the bar. He'd talk to me or the other bartender about her, about how beautiful she was, about what she was probably like, and all we'd say was, "Why don't you walk over and say hello?" Drove me nuts. The other bartender said this had been going on for 2 years already, so I missed most of it.

But I was there the night the guy finally screwed up his courage. He introduces himself, they sit down and have a little chat. Thirty minutes later, he's back. She leaves, and on her way out, she gives him a little wave. He nods. That's all. I say, "What's that all about?" He says, "She's not my type."

So what can I say, Greg? You've got a thing for a girl on TV who went to school to learn how to read a TelePrompTer. Television "journalists," by and large, are idiots. Those people don't know anything except how to look like they know something. So the chances are, you have something going in your head that'll never happen back on planet Earth. My advice: Write her a note. Then show up at some mall event or wherever she gets sent by the station. Introduce yourself. Then turn the TV back on and see if she waves. Chances are, you'll just nod off.

How to Say "Beer" Everywhere

Don't just ask for beer. Ask for one of these.

AUSTRALIA: Cooper Ale, Foster's
CANADA: Moosehead Lager
CHINA: Yixing
DENMARK: Carlsberg Elephant
ENGLAND: Guinness (yeah, I know, but it's still the best beer you can get in England)
FRANCE: Stella Artois (not a great beer, but nothing feels quite as right as saying "Stella" with meaning)
GERMANY: Becks Beer
KENYA: Tusker
IRELAND: Smithwick's and Guinness
ITALY: Nastro Azzuro
MEXICO: Corona Extra
POLAND: Krakus Zywiec
SOUTH AFRICA: Castle Lager
SPAIN: Cruzcampo
SWEDEN: Spendrups Old Gold
SWITZERLAND: Hurlimann Premium
THAILAND: Singha

Then there's Belgium. I don't know what it is about those Belgies, but they make great beer. It doesn't matter. If you get to Belgium, just say "beer," and you'll do all right.

Chests,
Hairy

I guess sometimes a guy just has to get off his chest what he's got on his mind.

Dear Jimmy,
   This is a serious question. If I shave my chest hairs, will they grow back hairier? Thanks. Please withhold my name.

—Name withheld

No, Jon, they won't. But they will grow back slowly. In the meantime, you'll be a scratching fool.

Why do you want a thicker chest rug? It's a crazy idea. I knew a guy once who wanted to grow hair on his head. So every day, he rubbed his scalp with vitamin E. It had no effect on his scalp at all. But his shoulders grew hairy epaulets and the stuff started sprouting out of his ears. It was disgusting.

Take what you're dealt and work with it. That goes for bald guys or short guys or skinny guys or guys with naked chests. If you're so obsessed with your looks that you're willing to do something as nuts as shaving your chest, then shaving your chest won't solve your problem. Nobody's perfect, Jon. Not even me. And if you get so wrapped up in covering your shortcomings that you start doing weird stuff like chest-shaving, all you're going to do is make sure everybody notices them.

Christian Charity,
the Soul of

Pass your own hat first.

Dear Jimmy,

My best friend's wife asked me to talk to my friend about not giving money to their church or to charity until they pay off their credit cards. They're about $20,000 in debt. What do you think?

—Oscar, San Diego

Churches and charities both collect money from people who have it, subtract what it costs to run the office, and give the rest to the poor or needy. That would be your buddy. He should become his own United Way for a while. When he's even again, he can start giving money to good causes. Until then, he's the best cause he knows. Explain this to him. If he still feels like he has to give away money he owes to others in order to make himself feel good and holy, tell him that, technically, that's called "stealing" and hand him a Bible. Tell him there's a rule against it in there someplace.

Cohabitation,
Downside of

The rule here is simple: Women. You can't live with 'em. Unless you marry 'em.

Dear Jimmy,
  She asked me to move in, Jim. I am not sure that I want to—how do I deal with this?

—Rob, Tulsa, Okla.

Two guys walk into my bar. First guy says, "Give me a drink, Jim. I'm breaking up with my girlfriend and I can't go home." Second guy says, "Give me a drink, too, Jim. I moved in with my girlfriend and I don't want to go home."

So the way I see it, you have a choice. You can tell her the truth, which is that you aren't ready to share a roll of toilet paper with the woman you love, or come see me and complain about your home life. If you need something to cushion the blow, try this: I read somewhere that couples who shack up before marriage are less likely to have kids, less likely to get married, and more likely to get a divorce if they do get hitched. Frankly, I'm hoping you move in. I could use the business.

Competition,
Friendly or Otherwise

*There's a big difference between who's the better man
and who's the best man.*

Dear Jimmy,
  I have a problem. It seems every time me and my
buddies go out to a bar or club, we end up setting our
sights on the same woman and we each end up trying
to battle it out to see who gets her. This sometimes
puts strains on our friendship. How do we all have a
good time going out and still not backstab each other
over a woman?

—Julio, Austin, Tex.

You're not fighting over women. Who ends up
with the girl is just the way you're keeping score
in a different game. Let's call it "How Insecure
Am I?" Here's how to play: You and your friends
go to a bar someplace. You decide which of you
has the most to worry about—like which one of
you is dumbest and which one of you is ugliest
and all that. There are two ways to decide. One
way is to vote. The other way is to let a bunch of
girls in a saloon vote for you. That'll tell you who
the losers are.

  But there's a different way to play this game.
These are your friends, right? So, Julio, why not see
how many bar-bims you can fix your amigos up
with? You'll win every time.

Dating,
Laws of Expense-Sharing in

I hate check-splitters.

Dear Jimmy,
   Maybe you could settle a bet. A woman who asks out a man is not only required by law of dating to pick the activities for the date but also to pay for those activities. Am I correct? But if a man asks a woman out, it's the other way around. Is that right, too? When do you split the expenses?

—Jerome, St. Louis

You split the expenses when you're too broke to pick up the check by yourself. I've had it with that. When men do it, it makes me want to dry-heave: You end up with no tip and a couple of guys squabbling like my battling aunts over five bucks. Take it someplace else.

Now, as for the first part of your question, here's what I think: Any woman bold enough to ask a guy out should be bold enough to pay, too. Obviously, if a man is doing the asking, he's the one who's going to pay. A man and a woman going out and splitting expenses is too unisex for my taste.

Death,
Explaining to Kids

It's there, like the big red exit sign back by the men's room.

Dear Jimmy,
My dad has cancer, and the doctor gave him less than 6 months to live. Should I tell my 10-year-old son the whole truth? Should I tell him that his grandpa is dying, or would it be easier on him to find out when it happens?

—Alex, Baltimore

Sounds tough, Alex. My grandfather died when I was 11, and I knew about it. The old guy gave me a silver dollar the day before he passed on. I still have it.

Here's what happened: My dad took me and my brothers to church. There was no mass going on or anything. He just took us there and made us all line up in a pew. Then he tells us he doesn't know beans about God. He says, "I'm just a man." But he tells us the universe is infinite, our lives are part of it, and there's something even bigger than all of us behind the whole business. He says, "I don't know what happens after you die, but I do know this: Grandpa is going to find out."

That's how he told us. For some reason, it made it okay, like it was part of some exciting adventure. And I guess it is. Ten-year-olds live for adventure. Tell him your dad's dying for it.

Death,
Family Quarrels and

Nobody's left to break up the siblings' slugfests.

Dear Jimmy,
I come from a big family (four brothers, two sisters). Two years ago, my father died, and last summer, Mom followed. We all seemed to pull together to get past this until it came time to settle the estate. Now we're at each other's throats. It's like a war. My brothers and sisters and I barely speak to each other. My oldest sister thinks she should run everything, and my brothers are teaming up to get things done their way. How do we call a truce?

—Tom, Wilmington, Del.

My place is the first place everybody stops after the funeral, so I hear about this stuff a lot. Plus, I have a big family, too, and we've been through this ourselves. Here's what worked for us. One of us (I'm not saying who) was trying to do what it sounds like your sister is doing. He figured that if he made up the rules, he'd win the game.

It got pretty ugly until my brother the priest pointed out that by arguing over who got the dining room table and the china, we were putting a price on our family. He said to one of my other brothers, "Look, as far as I'm concerned, you can have whatever you want. But make sure you can afford it." Trading a brother for a set of plates suddenly seemed pretty stupid.

Then he said something even smarter. He sat us all down and said that we were trying to settle old debts by seeing who could get away with giving orders and who would fight to not follow them. We all listened to him because he had taken himself out of the picture. The guy's a priest, for crying out loud. All he asked for was Mom's Bible and a few photographs. So he had this enormous standing as somebody with no vested interest.

You be that guy. Sit everybody down and tell them you want those two trinkets and those three photographs and that's all, except for one other thing: an agreement that you let an independent person settle the estate for you. It'll cost a bit, but it won't be as expensive as losing a whole family over a bunch of secondhand pots and pans.

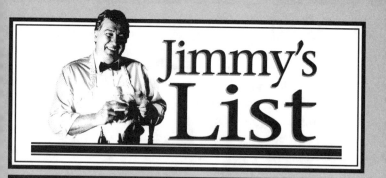

Jimmy's List

Reasons Why You Can't Live on Beer Alone

You'd think that, at a hundred calories or so a pop, you'd be too full to eat after a few brews. But getting drunk makes you hungry. Here's why.

1. BEER STIMULATES YOUR APPETITE. It doesn't satisfy it. All alcoholic drinks do that. That's why cocktail hour comes before dinner hour.

2. BEER LOWERS YOUR BLOOD SUGAR. And that makes you feel really hungry. Diabetics, beware.

3. BEER MAKES YOU PISS. It makes you want food, especially salty food.

4. BEER MAKES YOU PISS BEER. The stuff goes down the drain before your brain has time to say "full!"

5. IT ONLY TAKES ONE HAND TO DRINK A BEER. It only takes one hand to eat.

Dogs,
Why They're Man's Best Friend

Two words every man should understand: "Down, boy."

Dear Jimmy,
  Last weekend, my best friend, who is seriously involved with a great girl, strayed from the straight-and-narrow at a party with an ex-girlfriend. This got me upset enough that I left the party, only because he's on a super path with his girlfriend and they have a great future ahead of them. He knows I was pissed, but he thinks I'm mad only because he got laid and I didn't. I just want the best for him and he's putting that in jeopardy, as well as our friendship. How do I knock some sense into his head without it turning into a grudge match?

—Lou, Atlanta

If a guy like you wants a best friend, I say buy a dog. They're easier to train, you can control them completely, and they won't let you down.

  With me on this? My point is that you have to accept your buddy for what he is. He made a mistake. Now you have the right to spout off with your opinion—and in fact, I think one of the great things that a friend does is try to show his pal where he thinks he's making a mistake. But once you do that, he's got to be on his own. If what he ends up doing is something you don't think a friend of yours should be doing, then he's no friend of yours, and no amount of manipulation or persuasion or anything else will ever make him one.

Downside,
Getting Past Your Own

Nothing's a big deal unless you say it is.

Dear Jimmy,
I just lost my driver's license for a year. How do I get past the I-don't-have-a-car hurdle with the ladies?

—Ben, Grand Rapids, Mich.

Let me explain it this way. These two guys always come into my place together, and each has a problem. The first guy gets clumsy after a drink or two. The second guy has a brother who's in jail for killing two people. One night, I'm watching them hit on two women. The first guy is talking and he knocks his drink into his crotch, but he tries to ignore it and just keeps talking, like maybe she didn't notice. She finally looks at him like he's a freak and says, "Doesn't that bother you?" Then she makes up an excuse to get away from him. Meanwhile, his friend is telling tales about his killer brother to the other lady, and she's laughing away, having a great time.

Not having a license is like having a drink in your lap, Ben. You can't hide it, so don't try to stall or keep it a secret. Your only bet is to get it out in the open, and fast. But make it a by-the-way kind of joke thing. Like a brother who kills people. If you can make her laugh it off, you're home free. And she's driving.

Duty,
Fulfillment of

Absence makes the heart grow fonder—unless it's without leave.

Dear Jimmy,

I've been married for 2 years. I am in the military and have to go away from time to time to serve on various special assignments. My wife does not trust me. I go out with my buddies and they all tell me I'm stupid to be married. I'll be gone for 2 months the next time, and I plan on leaving and not coming home. I think my friends are right. I am stupid to believe that we can stay married with my being gone all of the time. We're not right for each other, I guess.

—G. I. Billy, San Diego

Hold it! I just thought of something! Your wife doesn't trust you because you trust your friends, and your friends are jerks. Just call it a Jimmy hunch. But think about these two questions: Why wouldn't she trust you, Billy? And just who's telling you you're not right for each other? If the answer to both of those questions is "the idiots I drink with," then you have your answer. You have the right to tell your friends to butt out of your marriage.

So here are your marching orders: Ditch your friends. Do your duty. Serve your country. Honor your wife. If you can't do one or more of these things, then get an honorable discharge, no matter which you choose. But don't just up and desert. That's what cowards do.

Education,
the Value of a Good

You don't know what you don't know.

Dear Jimmy,
   I'm stuck. I'm 22 years old, and I've been married for over a year now. My wife drives me insane. She's bitchy, a slob to live with, and she's ultra-sensitive, which makes it hard to approach her with things that are bothering me about her. I think about leaving her all the time. So what should I do? Should I quit, or should I try to stick it out?

—Tim, Orlando

Learning to live with a woman is like learning how to do brain surgery. It takes years of frustrating study before you have the slightest damned clue as to what you're doing, and chances are, along the way, somebody's going to get hurt. At the year-and-change point, you're only at the beginning of your internship, Tim, and, by the way, so is she. In fact, she probably has a long list of second thoughts regarding you right now. It's natural. But trust me on this point: Unless she's throwing steak knives at you, she's no more bitchy and messy and oversensitive as the next woman you'd meet. At 22, you don't know this. At 27 or 30, you will. So stay in school, and whatever you do, don't have kids until you're ready to graduate. That's my advice.

Fatherhood,
Financing of

You ask me, the money's the easy part.

Dear Jimmy,

I'm in my late thirties, and after trying for a long time, my wife got pregnant. I'm happy, of course, but she's making it rough. To make a long story short, she wants to stay home with the baby. We're a professional couple. On both salaries, we do great. But if she quits her job, we'll be in the poorhouse before the baby gets to kindergarten. How do I convince her not to be so selfish?

—Stefan, Los Angeles

Did I miss something? She's *selfish*? Where I'm working now, I'm surrounded by offices. Every day, at happy hour, I see a bunch of working moms and dads belting back martinis or whatever's in style. They're regulars—they're talking kids, talking day care, talking this and that, and tipping large. I like it. But you can't tell me that these people are ware-housing the brats because they need the money, can you? Get out of here. They're slamming the kid into day care because, as any drunk will tell you, it's a lot more fun to hang out in an office than it is to chase babies.

Your wife has the cockamamy idea that being a mother means spending time with a kid. Nuts? I don't think so. She's not being selfish, bud. You are. So pretend like you know what it means to be somebody's dad: Move to a smaller house, trade the Mercedes for a 2-year-old minivan, cut back your expenses, and stop blowing a hundred a week at happy hour. Believe me, you can afford to buy your kid a childhood. Sounds like you accidentally mar-ried the right woman. Now raise the right kid.

Fathers,
Know-It-Alls Who Are

They're not even safe at home

Dear Jimmy,

My 8-year-old son is a natural athlete. This year, he played Little League ball. I know a little about baseball, having played 2 years of semi-pro. I wish I could have coached his team, but I was busy. Unfortunately, the guy they did get to coach is an idiot. He doesn't know the first thing about baseball. My boy tells me some of the bonehead blunders the guy makes during the games, and I really see red. His incompetence is starting to hurt my son's future. I'm afraid to go to one of the games because I might blow a gasket. I don't really want to humiliate the schmuck in front of everybody, but I have to do something. How do you think I should handle it?

—Rick, Los Angeles

Hey, champ. So you heard secondhand what a lousy job this guy's been doing, right? My advice is to go and see for yourself. But not just for a few minutes some Saturday afternoon. No. Check out the guy like you were a private eye. In fact, do a little inside work: Go to every game and every practice. Get the goods on the guy by signing up to help out with the coaching. That way, you'll be able to document every bonehead blunder the guy makes. I know you're busy, but your son's future's on the line, right? There's only one way to handle bum coaches like that. Do it yourself.

Fathers,
the Lies They Tell Themselves

They make this stuff up as they go, I guess.

Dear Jimmy,
  I'm doing something that I swore I never would: After 5 years of marriage and having a 2-year-old kid, I am having an affair. It's the old story: The marriage wasn't great, and a co-worker became a sympathetic ear. Now I'm in love with this woman and can't live without her, but I love my kid with all my heart. I might be a bastard for cheating, but I'm a damn good dad and will not do anything to hurt my boy. What should I do?

—Lawrence, Philadelphia

This reminds me of the guys who say that they're glad they're not alcoholics—as they cash their paychecks for another round. You've already done something to hurt your boy, genius. You cheated on his mother. You put your interests ahead of his. You're lying to yourself and to him and to your wife because it was easier to start a new thing with the ear lady than to fix what was wrong at home. If you want to be a good dad, be a good husband first, because if you break up your marriage, you'll be a bad dad, no matter what you think.

Flow,
Going against the

When life's too easy, it's too late.

===

Dear Jimmy,
How do you know if your life is settling?

—Patrick, Toronto, Canada

For one thing, you're dead.

Let me explain that. See, settling is like early retirement, if you ask me. I don't want to count how many men I've worked with who have gone that route. But I tell you what, once they settle for not working, for a condo in Florida, for old age, then they die. Sometimes, it takes them a while to kick. Sometimes, they go right away. They all tell a zillion and one lies about why they're doing what they're doing. But the truth is, when they settle, they're settling for death, not for life.

The deal with living is that it's a continual struggle against gravity. Settling is kind of the default state of all inanimate objects. That's why, at a certain age, even standing up is a rejection of settling. That might sound kind of glum, but it's okay, really. Struggling, fighting, trying to make it all work—that's the condition of life. That's the deal you make. In exchange for living, you have to keep up the good fight. Once you stop, once you surrender, once you settle, you're a goner.

Friends,
What They're for

As long as you have a friend, you're never alone, right? Wrong.

Dear Jimmy,
I'm a married man (not happily, mind you, but married nonetheless), and I have this problem: My best friend just happens to be a woman, and I think I've fallen in love with her. On one hand, I have my obligations to my wife to be faithful, but on the other hand, I have my obligation to myself to be happy. Neither my wife nor my best friend knows what I'm going through. What do I do?

—Dan, Chicago

Hey, what are best friends for? Reminds me of guys who drink until they don't even know they're drunk. Then they get up and fall flat.

Now, take you. You've got quite a movie going here, right? Yes, you have a problem you can't take to your wife. So start by taking it to your best friend. Say, "Look, I've got this thing where I think I deserve to be happy no matter what promises I've made to other people, including the woman I married. I want to ditch her because she doesn't make me happy anymore. Should I just go for it, or what?"

She might be a little put off, so you'll have to explain that when you married your wife, you were on this happiness quest, too, but now you have different ideas about happiness. Be sure to tell your friend that you've "grown," because everybody knows that growth is good, and most people are willing to believe that it's something you can continue doing into your thirties and forties and beyond, especially if you explain that happiness isn't something you just want for yourself. Tell her it's an obligation—that you have a *duty* to be happy.

Now, once you get all this laid out to your best friend, and you're sure that she gets it, tell her that she's the lucky target of your deeply felt sense of obligation. Who knows? Maybe she didn't know what you're going through, and just thought you were friends, in which case you lose her as a best friend. Or, maybe you and your best friend are thinking alike, in which case you lose a wife. In this country, a guy can have as many friends as he wants. But he only gets one wife. You figure it out.

Friendship,
with Former Girlfriends

With ex-lovers like this, who needs friends?

Dear Jimmy,

Recently, my girlfriend of about 2 years broke up with me. A week later, she was in a relationship with a guy from work that she hung out with a lot when we were still together. She says she wants to be best friends, but it tears me up to know that she loves someone else. Do I have a right to be angry, and should I try to be her friend, even though it hurts so much?

—Jack, Dallas

Of course not. Tell her that you aren't friends; you're kaput lovers. Big difference there, J. Why do women think love is some weird form of friendship? It's a different animal. And it is perfectly all right to tell somebody who reached down your throat and did a heart-ectomy on you that you don't have one shred of interest in being her pal, thanks.

Girlfriends,
the Value of Old

Want to make your girlfriend look beautiful? Find her a new boyfriend.

Dear Jimmy,
  I was engaged to this girl for 2 years. Then I dumped her. Now I see her dating another guy, and it is getting to me. What should I do?

—Steve, Redondo Beach, Calif.

I'm working for this guy once, and he sees an ad in the paper where they're auctioning off a bunch of saloon stuff: sinks, coolers, all that. So the owner of the bar says to me, "You go, and if you see a good deal, bid on it and bring it back." I tell him I don't know anything about auctions, but he sends me anyway. I get there and I'm watching them sell this junk—and I mean junk—for twice what anybody in their right mind would pay for it. So I say to this guy standing next to me, "How do they get prices like that for this stuff?" The guy says, "That's how it is at an auction. The stuff's worth whatever somebody's willing to pay for it."

  When you "dumped her," as you so eloquently put it, you were telling her she wasn't worth the time and effort you were paying her. Now, she's found a higher bidder, and you're thinking maybe you dropped out too soon, right? You're wrong. She's worth to you just what you thought she was worth. She's worth more than that to some other guy. That's the way the auction goes.

Big Bladder Tricks

Nothing breaks my heart like seeing a shy guy duck into a crowded john on a Saturday night—and come out 2 minutes later looking like the Michelin Man. Here's how to make every trip to the can count:

1. WATER WORKS. Turn on a tap. Or, if there are already a million guys making dancing water, close your eyes and pretend you're pissing in the shower.

2. MIND-BODY TRICKS. Think of something relaxing. Or think of something you do effortlessly—sinking a putt, or making a layup.

3. NO TIME-OUTS. Give it all the time you need. Nobody's timing you. Thirty seconds might seem like a lot to you, but it's nothing to God.

4. WAIT FOR A STALL. This isn't science.

5. TRY TO FART. Hey, be careful in there! But it works.

Haircut,
How to Get a Good

Look for a good sign.

=======================================

Dear Jimmy,
   I know this isn't the kind of question bartenders usually get, but let me try anyway. I am 32 and I'm ready to give up on finding a decent hair salon. I either leave looking like somebody tried too hard or looking like a guy trying to look like a teenager. What's the secret word I can use to tell the stylist what I want?

—Jules, Boston

You're the one trying too hard. I see it all the time. Some guy comes in here looking for a way to impress himself. So he orders a Tarkhuna with pepper. Now, I know Tarkhuna's a great vodka with an herbal twist from Soviet Georgia. But I also know you haven't been able to get a bottle of the stuff this side of the Black Sea for at least 5 years. If the guy knows what Tarkhuna is but doesn't know that, then who's he trying to fool? Asking for that in a neighborhood bar is just stupid.

   Same with asking a stylist to cut your hair. You're not Tom Selleck. So don't put on airs. Go to a barber shop. Barber shops are the last bastion of manliness allowed in America. Ask for Al. Tell Al to cut your hair, but for God's sake, don't tell him your name is Jules. You'll leave looking and smelling like a man, not like some yuppified climber who can't dress without a clue from the Gap. Hair stylists for men? Sure. How about a trim and a spritzer?

Heartbreak,
Recovery from

It's like phenomenal diarrhea—really interesting to the person experiencing it, not quite as fascinating to everybody else.

Dear Jimmy,
What's the best way to get over a failed long-term relationship, short of becoming a priest or doing something drastic?

—Brian, Palm Harbor, Fla.

What's wrong with becoming a priest? My brother's a priest. On the other hand, at the "drastic" end of things, Dr. Kevorkian and half the voters in Oregon might say, "Feeling some pain? Have we got an alternative for you."

If I had a "demographic" for the booze business, you'd be in the middle of it. St. Patty's, New Year's Eve, and breakups seems to be the red days on the calendar of every amateur drunk in the world. So I know a bunch of guys in your shoes, walking around wounded, like miserable vets, complaining about the true love who broke their hearts.

The truth is, if you're still feeling unhinged after a reasonable period, then the problem is you. You don't have to forget her; just get past her. Because if you can't get over her, you're not doing anything with your life. You've put everything on hold. Why? Because you want her to come fix you up, take care of you, and make you right again, which is why she bounced you like a bad check in the first place.

After a killer breakup, the only way to get a woman to walk toward you is to walk away from her. Give it 6 months. If you can't get over her by then, it's because you don't want to, and that's another problem altogether.

Historical Revisionism,
Contributing to

How the Russians invented baseball.

Dear Jimmy,
   About a year ago, I was secretly intimate with a co-worker. It was a brief affair. Then I changed jobs, moved from one city to another, and lost track of her. Now I find out that she is going to marry one of my best friends. At this time, he has no idea that I slept with his future bride. So which of these things do I do? Let him know about it prior to his marriage? Worry about him finding out after he becomes married? Don't worry about it and still be his buddy?

—Carlos, Dallas

You're wrong about one of these two things: 1) You slept with her. 2) He's one of your best friends.

I'm willing to bet on number two. I think you barely know this guy or you would have seen this train wreck coming long ago. I think this is some guy on the periphery of your social circle and that you're feeling pretty important right now. So now that we've got you honest, let's figure this out.

Should you let him know about it? No. He either knows already or it doesn't matter. Should you worry that he'll find out later? No. Should you still be his buddy? No. The guy doesn't want a buddy who used to do his wife. But here's what you can do. When you see them together for the first time, greet her as a friend that you haven't seen for a while. Be courteous, friendly, and polite but not familiar. Then, go on your way, and in the future, if you see either of them, give a friendly smile, but stay away. To these people, you're history that never happened.

Sometimes, the wildlife's working for the zookeeper.

Dear Jimmy,
   I am a middle-level manager who recently asked my staff to evaluate my performance. My evaluations were very positive, yet my supervisor informed me that one particular staff member (a recently divorced woman who no doubt needs a good romp) who gave me an exceptionally good review has been going to upper management to get me fired. The nature of my business makes it difficult to rid myself of this menace, but I feel that if I do not address the situation, she may become a cancer that will spread to the rest of the staff. I can't punch her and she's way too ugly to give a romp. What do I do?

—Ted, Baltimore

Caught between a rock and a hard place, huh? I mean, you can't give her a good punch and you can't give her a good romp, so what's a guy to do?

Tell me something. Do they teach punching and romping as managerial skills in business schools? Or tell me this. Do they pay you to think? Just in case the answer's no, do this for me for free: Think about how you're going to solve this mess. You have a choice of either helping this woman become a good and productive employee or figuring out alternatives to your punch-and-romp solution. Don't get me wrong, bud. I hate sexual harassment hysteria as much as the next guy. And maybe the dame's no good. But you better wise up fast. To "address the situation" here, all you need to do is be polite and professional. In other words, manage yourself and your attitude, and the rest will fall into place. Give her rope. If she's the villain, she'll hang herself. If you are, then she'll be giving you her own version of a punch and a romp.

Industry Standards,
New vs. Old Bars

The biggest bar trick of all is showing a profit.

Dear Jimmy,
I love my local, but I have this one question: Why is it always crowded in the front? The place is huge, but it seems like the biggest crowd is always just inside the door. I always wondered about this.

—Richard, Costa Mesa, Calif.

Modern bars are like those little rat mazes: They've been worked out by guys in labs who have never lifted a glass touched by a barman. Sounds like your bar is one of those.

The knot of people you see when you first walk in are congregated around a magical spot called *the point* by barroom designers. It's the spot you see first. It's usually close to the door, the focus of a lot of the bar's activity, and, despite the traffic jam, it's pretty easy to get to. A badly designed bar has the clientele scattered all over the place. That's okay if it's busy. But if it's not, the place looks empty.

There are two basic bar types. One is a *shotgun bar*. That's the traditional American bar—a long slab of oak running along one wall from front to back, with a *backbar*, usually mirrored, behind the bartender and where the booze sits. The other type is called a *U bar*—a big island in the middle of the room. Franchise joints like these because it's easier to do food and all that. As a bartender, I like working a shotgun bar. It creeps me out when half the people behind my back are drunk and sloppy. The other bad thing about a U? No backbar. Maybe I'm too much of a traditionalist, but I like a bar where you can grab a stool and a drink and not have to look into the face of another guy just like you.

One other thing: The restrooms are *always* in the back. Don't ask again.

Jealousy,
Consequences of

Green isn't a bad color, actually.

Dear Jimmy,

You have to help me out. My girlfriend used to flirt with a lot of guys and I'd get jealous. She told me to trust her or leave. So, wanting to save an awesome relationship, naturally, I trusted her. Next thing I know, she goes on a trip with her university and tells me she slept in a bed with another guy, but that nothing happened. I got jealous, so she dumped me. Is there a way that I can make this better? I didn't mean to behave the way I did; it's just that I had a bad weekend, and I snapped. What is your best advice?

—Colin, Los Angeles

Can I make it better? Can I make *what* better? There's nothing there.

Let me explain to you what happened. The girl didn't like you anymore, so she dumped you. Now, let me explain to you how that happened. She accused you of thinking she was untrustworthy. Then, she did something untrustworthy. And when you told her she was untrustworthy, she told you to take a hike.

Now, let me explain why it happened. This is how women get rid of guys they don't like. They do something bad, but make you badder. Once you're the villain, they feel justified in sending you packing. Women always need justification for breaking a heart. Don't feel bad. The other way they do it is to tell you that you're just too nice.

Lies,
Living with

Some guys will shack up with anything.

Dear Jimmy,
I have been engaged to a woman for about a year. Now that things look like they are going to move to the next step, about seven of my friends came to me and told me that I should know that she had been running around on me. They said they never thought things would go as far as they have, so they thought what I didn't know wouldn't hurt me. I confronted her about it, and she denied it. I don't think my friends would all lie to me, but I want to believe her. Who do I believe? What do I do?

—Lyle, Fort Worth, Tex.

I could never figure those guys whose wives call them at my place, and they do this big "I'm not here" hand-gesture show. I never lie for them, but I don't rat on them, either. I usually just tell the truth, which is, "I'm busy." The mere fact that she had to call me looking for the guy tells the whole tale of that marriage. It makes me feel like a jerk, but at least I know who the real jerk is, and usually I cut him off and send him home. Believe me, the way some of these guys reek of booze and smoke when they leave my place, they aren't getting away with any lies. The fact is, their wives know they lie, and they live with it. For a while, anyway.

You're in the same boat. The fact that you had to ask her for the truth is the only fact you need to tell you this isn't the girl for you. Maybe she's pure as the driven snow, but if you don't trust her one hundred percent now, when nothing's at stake but your feelings and a small piece of jewelry, you're going to be living in hell when you add a mortgage and some kids to the deal.

Love,
the Language of

"How do I love thee? Let me count the ways . . ."

Dear Jimmy,
  What is the best way to tell a woman you have the hots for her?

—Christopher, Cleveland

Try friction. Rubbing up against her in the subway is always effective. I'm sorry, pal. If where you're starting with a woman is a consideration of your hots, then you're probably not going to get very far. But if you want her to like you for the sensitive, caring man that you probably are, try demonstrating your hotness by being interested in what she has to say and how she thinks. If she's great-looking, and I guess she must be, then a small compliment is enough. After that, simply *act* as though she has what it takes to blow your libidinal thermostat. See what I'm saying? If you want a girl to know you like her, then act like you like her.

Love,
Tough

Never hold hands with a jumper.

Dear Jimmy,
I can't seem to stop the lady in my life from overindulging in the grape. She's a good person, except when she drinks, and then all hell breaks loose. She needs AA but she won't go. Should I dump her if she refuses to get help?

—Wayne, Wilmington, Del.

Of course you should dump her if she refuses to get help.

That sounds heartless, I guess, but look. I see more than your average number of drunks where I work. Something about a bar just attracts them. But they all have this one thing in common: If I didn't throw them out, they wouldn't stop drinking until they wanted to. Or until they died. If your honey won't go to AA, send her packing now, because you can't save her. Only she can save herself. Trying to do it for her will kill her and kill you. End of story.

Market Research,
Learning from

Rule number one: Look for what works.

Dear Jimmy,
Two years ago, my girlfriend kissed my best friend and I was really pissed, but I got over it. Now, I just found out that they were actually in a hot tub and not wearing anything. Also, there were three of them—my girlfriend, my best friend, and some other girl. I have built a great relationship with my girlfriend and to hear this, well, it makes me sick. What should I do?

—Justin, Toronto, Canada

Three things you should do:

1) Get a hot tub.
2) Don't marry your girlfriend.
3) Ask your best friend what the trick is.

Martinis,
the Perfect Version

I put three classic drink recipes in this book. This is another one.

Dear Jimmy,
How do I make a great martini?

—Jamal, Chicago

Order one from me. Or, get yourself some nice martini glasses and follow this recipe.

Fill the martini glasses with ice to chill them, then set them aside with the ice still inside. Get a big tumbler (10 ounces) and fill it with ice. Pour a shot of Martini Extra Dry vermouth in there—count 1-2 and stop pouring—and let it trickle down the ice into the bottom of the glass. Then add two shots—that's 1-2-3-4—of a reasonable gin. At the moment, my well has a bottle of Booth's in it. That'll work. If you're James Bond and want it more potent, stir this with a fork for 15 seconds. To make it extra cold and weaker, cover the top of the tumbler and shake it vigorously for 10 seconds. Just don't agitate it for more than 30 seconds, or the ice will melt and ruin your drink. Now, toss the ice out of the martini glasses, and strain the liquid from the tumbler into each glass; use your finger if you don't have a bar strainer. Squeeze a thin lemon wedge into each, and then swab the pulp around the drinking edge. Toss in the spent lemon rind—or those damn olives—only if your guest says she wants it. Putting onions in any drink is ridiculous, by the way, so don't ask.

Men,
Lying and Cheating

. . . and usually getting caught. Why do we bother?

Dear Jimmy,

Help me, Jim. I slept with the stripper from my bachelor party, and now that I've been married for a year, I'm sick with guilt. Should I fess up to my wife?

—Ron, San Antonio, Tex.

I used to work in a hoity-toity lounge in the city. They had this piano player—a little guy, barely 5 feet tall. One night, the manager got caught with his hand in the piano player's tip jar. The piano player grabbed the guy's arm and slammed it over the edge of the jar, which broke, slicing the manager's wrist almost to the bone. The manager is practically bleeding to death, I'm calling for an ambulance, and the customers are flipping out, but the little guy still won't let go of the manager's arm. His face is red, his teeth are clenched, and he's saying, "Morty, don't screw with the entertainment."

You see what I'm saying here, don't you, Ronny? In your case, however, the deed is done. So here's the deal: You're going to keep the secret to yourself and live with the guilt. Because if you think you're going to make yourself feel better by getting this off your chest and putting it on your wife's back, you're wrong. You'll just have two miserable people and a miserable marriage.

The bottom line is, you screwed up. People screw up all the time. Get used to it, get over it, and try not to do it again with the next stripper at your next bachelor party. Before then, go see a doc and have a test for HIV, Romeo.

Jimmy's List

Jimmy's Barroom Wife-Screening Test

Let's say you're in my bar, and you meet a girl. After a few drinks, you think, "Hey. She might be the one." Before you pop the question, give her this test.

1. At a four-way stop, you tie with another guy approaching from the left. Plus, he doesn't quite stop all the way. Plus, you're late. Do you let the other guy go first?

2. Are you being treated on an outpatient basis for anything?

3. Do you know how to take care of a guy who never seems to be able to hold his liquor?

4. Do you admire guys who are poor but sensitive?

5. Do you think Garrison Keillor is funny?

6. If you had to choose between driving fast on an open road or talking to your best friend about her new guy on your cell phone in traffic, would you choose the gossip?

7. Would you rather be with a really smart dolphin right now?

8. Do you think there are no good men left out there?

9. Aren't cats *cute*?

10. I know we just met, but I think I'm in love. Wanna go to my place?

Now, give each "yes" answer 10 points and total it up. If the total is 10 or higher, forget her. It's the liquor talking.

Men,
What They're Good for

Tote that barge. Lift that bale.

Dear Jimmy,
I work in an office in which I am the only male. Most would see this as a gift from the gods, but I have a real problem with it. It seems that whenever there is any manual labor to be done, any box to be lifted, any wall to be repaired, anything like that, I'm given the job. When any of the women ask for days off or shift changes, I'm the one left holding the bag. Once, when we remodeled, I had to move our entire office by myself. Normally, I wouldn't mind except that I am never asked, I am told. In theory, I am a supervisor in customer service. In practice, I'm a day-laborer. Is it me, or might this be reverse sexism?

—Mike, Pittsburgh

Both. It's you, but it's also sexism. It's a tough call, Mike. I once had a situation like this. A guy was soaking up his disaster-of-the-day at the bar one night. It was jammed in there. Next to him is a pregnant woman, standing. She was drinking water and talking to a friend, but after an hour or so, you could see it was getting to her. So I said to the guy, "Hey, mind giving the lady your stool?" Well, the guy lit into me. I was just about to give him the heave-ho, when she started in on me, too, saying she didn't ask for my help and if she'd wanted it, she'd have asked for it. I just walked away. I think they were both jerks, but I was, too, because I should have asked before I jumped into it.

You should do all the things that you'd expect a man to do. But you should be asked. If you aren't, then simply tell it straight: Say you will do whatever is required of a gentleman, but you expect to be treated like one.

Miracle Cures,
Role of Sex in

Sometimes, it's the touch of a child. Sometimes, a rainbow on a misty morning. Sometimes, a kiss on the lips from a virtual stranger.

Dear Jimmy,
   I split up with my girl about 3 years ago, and I've had a tough time talking to women ever since. Any suggestions on how to get back on the horse?

—George, Boston

Excuse me? Did somebody say "horse"? I just don't see much of a future in equestrian analogies, frankly. Don't ask me why, but women hate the idea of being "mounted" and "ridden." So maybe there's your problem with talking to women. On the other hand, partner, if you mean you're just shy with the ladies, then I thank God you don't drink in my bar. Everybody you know must be sick of hearing you whine, and you're probably sick of thinking about the breakup that got you to this place. So do what every other guy does: Instead of hitting on a woman you're actually attracted to and being afraid that she'll say no, hit on some broad you don't give a damn about. If she says no, just keep asking different women you couldn't care less about. That way, your biggest fear is that one of 'em will say yes. And eventually, one will. The good news: She'll be grateful. The great news: You'll be cured.

Mixology,
for Idiots

I included three classic drink recipes in this book. Unfortunately, there are few classic drinkers left. This is for all the others except women.

Dear Jimmy,
  I've become somewhat of a Singapore sling addict. When I go out, though, each different place has a totally different sling. I know that each bartender will have his own style, but I've tasted everything from what was like fruit juice to vodka straight up. What exactly is in a Singapore sling? And how do I know if I'm getting a good one?

—J. P. G., Boston

To make a Singapore sling, mix a couple of ounces of gin with an ounce of cherry brandy, an ounce of lemon juice, some club soda, and a single ice cube.

To make a *good* Singapore sling, hold the cherry brandy, hold the lemon juice, hold the soda, hold the ice. Drink the rest.

Mixology,
Women's Drinks

I put three classic drink recipes in this book. This isn't one either.

Dear Jimmy,
What's the best drink to make for a woman?

—H. T., Albuquerque, N. Mex.

Go sweet. Women like drinks that taste innocent, but that would choke a man. For example, a chocolate martini. Take a half-ounce of vodka, a half-ounce of crème de cacao, shake it up in a tumbler filled with ice, and strain into a chilled martini glass. Makes my skin crawl just thinking about it.

By the way, I never met a self-respecting man who would defile a drink that way, nor a good-looking woman who didn't love it.

Monogamy,
the Virtue of

Fidelity is easier once you realize you have nobody to cheat with.

Dear Jimmy,
  My girlfriend and I have broken up three times. I can never meet anybody else, so we keep getting back together. What's wrong with us?

—Edmund, Richmond, Va.

Us? Where did that come from? The other night, two guys were in here drinking. One guy got drunk. The other guy didn't. The drunk guy said, "Wow, how did we get so hammered?" Look around you, Edmund, my boy. You're what's wrong with that "us" of yours.

I had this happen with one of my brothers—I'm not saying which. He's working in Chicago and he meets a girl. He loves her, she loves him, but they fight day and night. So he decides it's over. How does he end it? By sitting her down and telling her, right? No. He takes a job in Mobile, Alabama. Why? Because he thinks southern girls are beautiful and he wants one. They are beautiful, but my brother isn't. So he's lonely and desperate. He calls the old girlfriend and convinces her to move to Mobile. Then he breaks it off again and buys a bar in El Paso. Six months later, he calls her again. Now they're married. His life is hell. But she's not the cause of it. He is, and you are, too. Look, if you've yo-yoed this girl back and forth as often as you say you have, it's because she loves you, and you obviously can't find anybody else.

So keep her, Edmund. Keep her, because she's probably the last dame on Earth who will want to see you with your pants down. Keep her, and the next time you want to end it, remember, she's taking your love life with her when she goes.

Moving,
Relocations and

The devil's in the details, and the details are in boxes.

Dear Jimmy,

My wife and I seemed quite happy until several months ago, when we went through our third career-related relocation. My wife's demeanor changed quickly, and now we have agreed to get a divorce. Although it is currently progressing amicably, I still find myself a bit stunned over the current scenario. We've been married for just over 3 years and dated for 6, but it looks like things are quickly drawing to an end. The funny thing is that my wife is treating this very matter-of-factly, with almost the same detachment one uses when one buys a new couch. What gives?

—Tim, Salt Lake City

I used to have a guy who'd leave 20, 30 bucks on the bar when he went home. He'd come in the next night, I'd put his money back in front of him, and he'd count it, add some to it, and do the same thing again. Every time he'd leave, I'd say, "Tommy, your money," and he'd always say, "You look after it for me." I hated that. I felt like he was taking me for granted, like all I had to do with my time was keep track of his cash. If he didn't count it, then I wouldn't have to count it, and we'd both be trusting each other. But as it was, I was the guy on the spot. So one night when he was heading for the door, I said, "Thanks for the tip, Tommy." The guy wheeled, came back, stuffed the money in his pockets, and never came back again.

I'm thinking that someplace along the way—maybe between relocations one and two—you left your marriage under the bed and just expected her to pack it up and bring it along. She didn't. Now it's lost. And the fact that you didn't notice it was gone before now doesn't leave much to be said.

Dedication always pays.

Dear Jimmy,
  I love hanging out in bars. Maybe that's why I have such a huge gut. How can I work on my abs without missing my counter time?

—Huey, Sacramento

You think you're kidding, but I actually know a good exercise you can do on a chair or even a barstool, if you've got a good sense of balance. I got this from a trainer when I was worried about my own gut. Here's what you do: Sit on the edge of a chair and grab hold of the seat on the sides, just behind your butt. Lean back a little and stretch your legs out so your heels are off the ground about the length of a dollar bill. Now, bend your knees and— real slowly now—raise your legs up toward your body, while leaning slightly forward to meet your legs as they approach your chest. Then, slowly drop them back down to where you started. Keep your abs tense all the time. Do this about 20 times, and you'll deserve a beer. Doubt if you could drink it, though.

Nice Guys,
the Slow Running of

It's not just that they finish last. It's that they get in the way of the rest of the pack.

Dear Jimmy,

I am an attractive man in my mid-thirties. I date attractive women. But every time, by the third or fourth date, the woman I'm with tells me she just wants to be friends. What can I do?

—Michael, Buenos Aires, Argentina

In my line of work, I see a lot of social dancing, if you know what I mean. The big question is, who is going to lead and who is going to follow? Trust me on this one: Women love it when you don't make it complicated. Because if you do, they'll uncomplicate it for you right away. So if you come on to a woman by acting like Mr. Nice Guy, that's what you'll be, probably forever.

So don't be a nice guy. Just be a polite guy. But most of all, be a guy. Be direct and unapologetic. The very first time you take her out, make sure she knows it's a date. Call it a date. Say, "I'd like to take you out on a date." Call the shots for the evening. Touch the small of her back as you walk. Open doors for her. Give her your best smolder. In other words, don't act like her friend. Act like her lover. And at the end of the night—trust me here, Mike—hold her head gently in your hands, tilt it up, and plant a kiss right on her lips. Not a quick peck, either. I mean a no-cousin, 3-second kiss. Hey, but no tongue. If she doesn't want romance and you do, don't give her a second chance, because she won't give you one. And that's okay. As my old man used to say, "Jimmy, you're a long time dead." And so you are.

Odds,
How to Figure the, Part One

Odds are, if you have to ask if you're doing the right thing, the answer's no.

Dear Jimmy,
I've been thinking about doing the nasty with an ex-co-worker. She's married, and I'm living with my girl-friend and our son. This ex-co-worker is one of the sexiest women I've ever been around. I get aroused just talking on the phone with her about work. I haven't been like this since I was 17 years old (I'm 34). I really want to sleep with her. Neither one of us says we're in-terested in leaving our partners. What are the odds? I need a straight answer.

—Don, Orlando

How about a straight question? I used to work in a tavern where we had to sell lottery tickets. I hated that. Put yourself in my shoes: You serve stuff to guys to make them stupid, then you watch them demonstrate just how stupid they are.

So what's your real question? You want the odds—on what? That you're an immature hound dog looking for your future in your shorts? I'd put that at about a million-to-one in favor. Or do you want the odds that this little retro-dalliance of yours will give you some big happiness payoff? You're better off buying a secondhand lottery ticket. Here's a sure thing: Marry your son's mother. Treat her with the respect the mother of your son deserves, despite the fact that she's with you. In other words, be a man, not a big kid. If you came into my bar with a question like that, I wouldn't serve you be-cause you're too dumb sober to be able to waste any smarts on a drink.

Odds,
How to Figure the, Part Two

Even at a trillion to one, there's always that one.

Dear Jimmy,
  I'm engaged to be married to a great girl. She isn't the most exciting woman on Earth, but she's one of the best. Lately, just for the heck of it, I've been flirting with this woman I met online. My girlfriend also spends a lot of time online for her work. I'm afraid I'll be caught. What are the odds?

—Frank, Columbia, Md.

When I first came to work at the place I'm at now, I was introduced to the bar's most famous customer. He was a guy who had been struck by lightning. I asked him about it, and he told me that it felt really strange. He said that he was disoriented for a month or something like that. Then, not 2 months later, he gets struck by lightning again! This time, it really laid him up, but he survived it. When he finally came back, he was twice as famous, so we gave him a little party, with lots of metal-tipped umbrellas and kites with keys and all that. A year later, he gets killed by a car while riding his bike in the middle of a national forest.

  I'm telling you this because you need to understand something about the way odds work. There are something like 20 million people online, so among all of them, your odds of being caught are 20,000,000:1, give or take. But there's only one of you and only one of your fiancée. She'll know when you're cheating, I swear it. So the odds of you being caught by her are 1:1. That's what I call a safe bet.

Office Parties,
Dumb Things Done at

Just because the boss pays for your drinks doesn't mean the boss is paying you to be stupid.

Dear Jimmy,
I got drunk at an office party and accidentally made a pass at a co-worker. Now, things at work are really awkward between us, and she's threatening to accuse me of sexual harassment. We used to be really good friends, but now, every day at work sucks. I really like my job, but I wonder If I should find a new one.

—Brady, Fort Lauderdale, Fla.

I like the "accidentally" part. You didn't mean to, right? Bonehead. Look, I'm assuming you already apologized to her in a big, big way. But if you didn't, go to her office, tell her you're one stupid sonuvabitch, and you're full-blown sorry for being such an insensitive ass to her. What you meant as a compliment came out really, really wrong. Don't actually say the words, "It was all my fault," since her lawyers might like that. But make her think she heard it, anyway. Tell her she'll get no more advances or leers or any of that nonsense from you, and you just want to forget the whole thing.

If she's still hostile after this—and you're genuinely being a decent, neutral guy to her—she's a no-good wench who likes having this over your head. And she holds all the cards here, sorry to say. Her lies are good as truth, her accusations good enough to convict you. Follow me? She has a loaded gun, and she's a lunatic that can't be disarmed. So if she won't accept your apology, you have no choice but to get far away from her. Another company works best. If you try to run after she pulls the trigger, you can forget about references.

Old-Fashioned,
the Perfect Version

I put three classic drink recipes in this book. This is the last one..

Dear Jimmy,
   What's the most classic drink for a man of distinction?

—Ed, York, Pa.

Whatever he likes, obviously. Me, I'd start with an old-fashioned. Put a couple of teaspoons of sugar syrup and three dashes of Angostura bitters into a low, wide-mouthed glass—they're actually called old-fashioned glasses. Stir with a spoon. Add some ice and 2 ounces of good rye whiskey and stir it again. Toss in a lemon twist and an orange slice for garnish. Drink two. The third time, leave out everything but the rye. Now you're making a drink for a *real* man of distinction.

Jimmy's List

Great American Sports Bars

A sports bar is what churches would look like if men were just now getting around to inventing religion. You've got your object of veneration (your team, of course), your kindly cleric (that would be me), a number of miracles (ninth-inning homers and all that) and your mystery liquid, the stuff that changes how you feel.

Call me an old believer. When it comes to that kind of religion, I admit I'm a traditionalist. I prefer smaller places where the game is the thing, not your large, hangarlike joints. But every now and then, I like mixing with the crowd, and if I were on the loose and needed to pop a brew and watch a quarter, here's where I'd do it.

1. BALTIMORE: ESPN. Kind of like a factory showroom, but very ultimate, as the lads say.

2. ST. LOUIS: Ozzie's. Ozzie Davis, that is.

3. NEW YORK CITY: Mickey Mantle's. Okay. You know all about it. But it's the Mick. It's New York.

4. CORAL GABLES, FLORIDA: Dan Marino's Bar and Grill.

5. CHICAGO: Sluggers, Hi-Tops, and The Cubby Bear. Think about it. Three huge sports bars for one losing team. There's a moral at the bottom of that pitcher someplace.

6. SAN FRANCISCO: Pat O'Shea's Mad Hatter.

7. WASHINGTON, D.C.: Champions. Of course, all the champs are from out of town, but hey.

8. PHILADELPHIA: Dave & Buster's. Lots of virtual-reality junk, too, if you're on the run.

Omens,
Reading

Even a lawyer deserves fair warning.

Dear Jimmy,

Got any advice on dating a 35 year-old-nurse with an 11-year-old daughter? I have met the daughter and we get along well, although she does not like me stealing a smooch from her mom. The father has been out of the picture for a number of years but still pays child support. I am a hardworking 31-year-old attorney who has no problem getting dates, but little experience with kids. I really admire my new girlfriend and like the sense of family around her, although she can drink too much at parties with her friends, which once led to a broken bone (hers) and me chasing off would-be Romeos who were looking to snag a sexy woman that had one too many. We have been dating for about a month. My friends think I am nuts. What am I getting into?

—H. K., Hartford, Conn.

Trouble. At least, that's what the early returns show. Where I come from, 35-year-old nurse-moms *set* broken bones, they don't get sloshed and break them. I'd think twice about her and give your friends a second listen. Who knows? Maybe she's just out of control. I see that kind of thing every day. But something about this smells. This is month one. Wait six more and drop me a note. Maybe you don't know too much about raising kids, but if you get involved with this woman, I have a strong feeling that you'll get two of them.

But don't blow her off on my say-so. In fact, let her help make the decision. Stop chasing off those Romeos. If she's not giving them her own keep-off sign when she's drunk, she's probably not long for you sober, either.

OPEC,
What We Can Learn from

Invisible forces shape the price you pay at the pump.

Dear Jimmy,
My wife and I have been together for 7 years. Our marriage has been great and our sex life has been fantastic—when she lets it happen. I work hard to make it easy for her to want sex, helping with the kids, doing laundry, offering her hot baths, anything that will show her how special I really think she is. I have had little success. Her libido is about half as strong as mine. What should I do?

—Roberto, Orange, Calif.

It's a good thing that somebody's keeping track, Roberto. But it's a better thing that you're the one doing it.

Want to know what's worse? When she wants more than you have to give. That's worse. Smart women understand this simple lesson and—I think it's instinct—figure out how to ration it the way the King of Saudi Arabia passes out gas and oil. Your idea of not enough may be her idea of just right.

If you're talking global shortage, however, it could be fatigue or a medical problem. It could also be those wonderful kids of yours that did it. Just as a matter of routine, she should see a family doctor to make sure there's nothing wrong inside. I knew a guy whose wife divorced him because she had a hormonal imbalance. When she got it fixed, they got back together. I've read they can slap testosterone patches on women to help them regain some of their sex drive. But what do I know? Ask the doctor if any medical issues are making her less interested in knocking boots with you. But let it be her choice to ask. Remember, half the sex you want is better than none—but much better than twice the sex you want.

Out,
Gross

It's like going native, I guess.

Dear Jimmy,
What's the worst drink to offer a woman?

—Phil, San Mateo, Calif.

There are three drinks that will make any woman with sense lose her lunch on the spot. One is that stupid pseudo-mescal with the worm in it. The other's a sake called Silver Gekkeikan. Comes with a 2-inch-long queen termite installed at the factory. The third is just one more of anything when she says she's already feeling sick.

Outdoors,
the Great

But don't bring it in here.

Dear Jimmy,

Every year, I go camping with three good friends. This will seem petty, but in 6 years, I've never been the one who builds the fire while everybody else sets up camp. I don't want to make a big thing out of it, obviously, but it is important to me to do this. How can I pull this off without looking stupid?

—Griff, Seattle

Here are a few things I've noticed in my 3 decades behind a bar.

- Guys who never get drunk, but decide to go on a tear, order boilermakers. Then they get sick, not drunk.
- No male over the age of 21 drinks peach brandy or any of those other fruit brandies, so even if my customer's got gray hair and drools, I card him if he orders this, and I'm always right.
- Guys who are out with a girl and trying to impress her will send back one of my martinis and tell me to "try again" or some other stupid thing. If I play along, I get a huge tip and the guy gets points. If I'm busy, I just stare at the guy until he disappears before my very eyes.
- Women under 28 drink Southern Comfort. Women over 28 who want a rich husband order mixed drinks using vodka, but specify Stoli. Humorless women order red wine. Nice girls drink spritzers.
- Any guy who whistles to get my attention has never been in a bar before.

I could go on with these things forever. But eventually, I'd come to this one, so let's just get to the point.

- Weenies who never go camping always want to build the fire.

It's a law of nature. It never fails. So next time, while you're pitching a perfect tent, warm yourself with the thought that whatever else you are, at least you're not the guy who's so insecure that he insists on building the fire. Then, forget you even had that thought and enjoy yourself.

Pants,
Who Should Wear Them

When nobody's in charge, everybody pays.

Dear Jimmy,
I have a high-tech relationship problem that you may be able to help me with. I bought my wife a computer nine months ago. Two days ago, I saw her off at the airport to meet one of her online male friends. He paid for her airline ticket to get there. Should I have said, "No—it's me or him," or do you believe in the old saying, "If you love something set it free"? I personally feel that it was selfish to leave me here to look after our three kids and work at the same time.

—Sean, Parma, Ohio

I'm a big believer in the if-you-love-something-let-it-go theory, so long as what you love is a bad cat. And I hate to be the first one to tell you, but that wedding you had was the it's-me-or-him moment. What were you thinking, man? What do you think would have happened if you'd said no? That she might have left you? Seems to me you're more concerned with juggling work and child care than you are with the fact that your wife is being flown around the country for other men's pleasure. Call your mother. Ask her to raise your kids. Sell your house. Either divorce your wife or start charging for her. You don't need my advice. You need a spinal transplant. Call a doc.

Paranoia,
the Truth about

What you don't know can't hurt you. What you think you know can be a killer.

Dear Jimmy,
How come my women always check out other guys when they're with me, yet other women never check me out when I'm alone? I know women love to flirt when they have someone to go home to, but how can I control this to my advantage?

—Brent, Los Angeles

I used to work a shotgun bar with no backbar mirror. It was miserable. You could never keep track of where your customers were, because they were always in motion. Then it dawned on me that the reason they all got up and moved around so much was because there was no mirror to reflect the rest of the bar, so the only way to see what was going on was to get up and look. Take you, for example. You don't think women are checking you out. Maybe you're right. Maybe you're wrong. But either way, you'll never know for sure since most women will never let you catch them stealing a peek. My advice: Act as if every woman in the joint has checked you out.

As for your dates looking at other men, you're only letting yourself see what you want to see, and since you're insecure, that's not a happy picture. Sure, Brent, when you're the bird in the hand, you'll naturally notice her eyes roving because you're looking in her face all night. How can you control this to your advantage? Be the bird in the hand.

Popping Champagne,
Elements of

When you know what you're doing, she's the whole show.

Dear Jimmy,
   I'm a working guy, and I don't usually get into a lot of fancy stuff. But I'm going out with a professional woman. We've gotten pretty serious, and I think it's time to show her that I'm not exactly a beer-drinking Neanderthal. I was going to take her to the movies, then afterward, we'd come back to my place for a little bubbly and I thought I'd propose. Any tips? I have to admit, I've never even bought a bottle of champagne, let alone opened one.

—Devin, Louisville

Yeah, sure. Skip the movie. Instead, build the whole evening around her. Go to a nice restaurant and let some professionals feed you, while you talk and listen. Order a nice wine; just tell the sommelier to bring you his suggestion.

   If you want a bottle of champagne, make sure it's really champagne, which is an imported wine from the Champagne region of France. I like a dry champagne, personally, so I'd look for "Brut" or "Extra Brut" and go for a known brand—Piper, Moët, or one of the other famous marks. Expensive, but worth it. The waiter will pour the first glass, offering you a small taste. Just sip and nod. When it's your turn to pour, do it slowly until the glass is about half-full, then hand the glass to her by the stem. By taking your show on the road, you leave all the details to the hired help—guys like me—so you can take care of the big job.

   If you insist on capping the evening back at your place, pop the question any way you want, but pop the bubbly like a pro. Chill the bottle in the icebox, not in an ice bucket. You don't want to be wrestling a wet torpedo. The object of the game here is to get the cork out of the bottle without breaking a sweat or a window. This should be an elegant, little gesture.

Put the bottle on a table and check out the top. Zip off the pull tab up there and peel back the foil. Now you'll see a little wire basket covering the top of the cork. See that little loop? Twist it counter-clockwise until it's loose. Hold the cork in place while you spread the wire away from the bottle's neck.

Now, take the bottle in your left hand (if you're a righty), like a football, with the top pointing up at about a 45-degree angle. If you try to take off the cork while the bottle is setting on the table, the thing will fire like a rocket right into your face. So hold the bottle with your left hand and hold the cork with your right and gently twist the bottle—while you hold the cork. Hey. I said *hold the cork*. The thing's under pressure and either it or the bottle could go flying. The only sound you should hear is a little "pop," not a big bang. You always know you're in an amateur bar when the counter help starts shooting off their cheap bubbly like somebody had just won the Little League World Series.

Now, that's out of the way, so tell me: What, exactly, is wrong with being a beer-drinker?

Prenuptial Agreements,
Wisdom of

A marriage vow—right there in front of a priest and God and your mother—to some guys, none of it means anything unless you have a lawyer to go with it.

Dear Jimmy,
My buddies keep telling me I should have my fiancée sign a prenuptial agreement. How do I know if I need one, and how do I ask her to go along with it?

—Tom, Beverly, Mass.

I once wrote out a prenup on a bar napkin because this guy wanted to marry a babe he'd been buying drinks for all night. He was a broker making six figures, and he thought she might soak him. So I wrote it, they signed it, I put it in the big brandy snifter next to the register, and, honest, 2 weeks later they were married. Turned out her old man owned a huge chunk of L.A. That was 3 years ago. Recently, she showed up and asked for the napkin.

So, before I venture an opinion, answer two questions. First, who are your buddies, and why are they telling you this? This counts because there are only four good reasons to make a prenuptial agreement, and they all have to be present: 1) you have to be really rich; 2) she has to be really broke; 3) you have to think there's a chance the marriage might fail; and 4) you have to think that she just might be a bloodsucker.

Do your buddies know something you don't?

Second, are you two going to have kids? If the answer's no, then get a prenup—from a lawyer, not a bartender—because you really have no reason to get married at all, so there's no reason to think you'll stay married. How to get her to sign it? Ask. If she says no, say no to her. But if the answer to the kid question is yes, then skip the prenup and figure that no matter what happens, it's going to turn out better for the wee tykes, the ones you'll have to support anyway.

There is another solution: Find a woman richer than you are, get her drunk, and marry her. But don't say a word to the bartender.

Jimmy's List

Bars and Blubber

Here's what your body is getting when you place your order:

Liquid Nutrition
Bourbon (or any 80-proof well drink) and soda: 65 calories

Glass of wine (any color): 85 calories

Light beer: 95 calories

A coffee drink with an ounce of booze in it: 100 calories, without the whipped cream

White Russian: 245 calories

Piña Colada: 329 calories and a stupid song you can't shake

Daiquiri: 422 calories

Food
Large bar pretzel: 35 calories or so

Slim Jim: 70 calories

Goldfish, a handful: 130 calories

Pizza, a slice: 140 calories

Onion rings, four: 220 calories

Hot wings, four: 280 calories

Peanuts, a handful: 336 calories

Nachos with all of Mexico piled on top: 570 calories

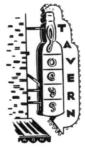

Promotions,
Friends Lost because of

The boss is a hard guy to like.

Dear Jimmy,
A group of us—five guys—have worked at the same company for a lot of years. We've stayed friends through thick and thin—until now. I recently received a double-jump, and I'm now at the VP level. Now my friends are giving me problems. I've tried to explain to them how hard it is to be doing what I'm doing, but it doesn't seem to matter. To make it all worse, they're letting me down on the job, I guess because they think I won't fire them. Any advice?

—Wolf, Paramus, N.J.

I once worked in a place in mid-Manhattan, maybe 15 years ago. I shared a shift with another guy and we became friends, more or less. Then the owners decided to make one of us senior bartender and offered it to me. I turned it down. What was it going to give me? But the other guy, he took it. I didn't say anything about the offer they'd made to me. Well, either he found out or it didn't matter, because almost overnight, he became insufferable. I couldn't stand it, and I quit.

Here's what he did that made it tough. He continually whined to me about how hard it was to make sure "his employees" (that would be me) understood the pressure he was under and how it was tough being on top and all that. The guy drove me nuts complaining about his promotion.

Here's what he should have done, and what you should do, too. Don't suffer over your success. It only makes people crazy. Just do your job. Leave all the psychology at home. Treat your friends like friends when you're not at work and treat them as co-workers on the job. If you start wearing a heavy crown, they won't be the only ones who'll want to see your head roll.

Questions,
Rhetorical

Sometimes, they're just asking.

Dear Jimmy,

    My wife and I have been married for almost a year-and-a-half now. After about the 1-year mark, she started posing questions that I don't know how to answer or even if I should try. For example, one time we were talking about her day. And then, without any warning, out of nowhere, she asked, "What would you think if I said I wanted to be a stripper?" Now how the hell am I supposed to answer that? What's going on, really?

—Brian, Destin, Fla.

Tell her that you'd personally be very proud if she became a stripper. Ask to preview her show. Suggest that she invite her co-workers home once a week so that the house would occasionally be packed full of surgically enhanced women. Then, start thinking up stage names for her, like Savannah or Vixxxen. She's not looking for answers, knucklehead. She's looking for fun.

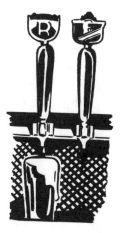

Real Life,
Identifying the Characteristics of a

When it comes to a life, the have-nots hate the haves.

Dear Jimmy,

I come from a small town in the Midwest. I have a best friend who has been my best friend since I can remember. After high school, we went our separate ways for a while. During that time, I went to college and he got married, had a couple of kids, and started working in a factory. After college, I took a 6-month contract in the Caribbean working for a cruise line. Once I returned, I had experienced so much and matured so much I fear I have nothing in common with him anymore. I can't talk about getting all these fantastic women because it only reminds him of his big mistake, and I can't talk about these wonderful career opportunities I have because I feel like I'm bragging to a guy who can't compete. The worst thing of all, though, is that he did this to himself. We all knew he had the potential to be much more than what he settled for. I'm never going to turn my back on him—hell, he's been there my whole life, practically. But what can I do to bridge this new gap between us? How can I relate to him again?

—Aaron, Kansas City, Mo.

I can see your problem right away. It's a toughie. Here's a way you two might be able to relate, now that your eyes have been so opened and everything. You ask him what it's like to be a man who's got an honest hard job, kids who think he's God, a woman with a checkbook with two names on it, and real respect for his friends, and you can tell him what it's like to have a tan, a box of funny Polaroids, 14 white polyester shirts, and herpes. Just let him down easy, pal.

Reboot,
Husbands, How to

Once upon a time, you couldn't get him to stop. Now you can't get him to start.

Dear Jimmy,
   I have a question that I am hoping you can answer for me. I have been married for 5 years and love my husband very much. He pays the bills and is very good with the children, but he is totally distant from me sexually. He never kisses me or hugs me and acts like I just work here. I was wondering how I can make him notice me. I love him and actually, I know he loves me also. Any suggestions would be welcome. We are not old, by the way. We're in our mid-thirties.

—Daisy, Hoboken, N.J.

Ever get this thing with your computer where you're using it normally and all of a sudden, it starts screwing up? No reason for it. It just goes south. I bought myself one of those computers and the first time it happened, I thought, "Oh, jeez, Jimmy, now you've really done it." So I asked one of my regulars, a guy who knows about computers, what it was all about. He told me the operating system gets corrupted after a while. He said there are lots of ways to fix it, but the easiest work-around was just to shut it down and start it up again. It's like giving it new instructions. So that's what I did. It works fine, and whenever it goes on the fritz, I know just what to do.

That old 486 of yours is having the same problem. He's shut down and he's waiting for new instructions. In the case of men and women, that means he's waiting to get your instructions, since all that men know how to do is try to follow the orders given to them by their wives (or women in general). I think the best way to tell him what you want is to make your expectations really clear. If you expect to get a cold shoulder, then that's what he'll do. But if you start acting like a woman who not only expects sex but thinks she's worth it, then he'll start paying attention. You don't need to say a word. Just act like a woman who likes sex, and your dreams will come true. If I'm not right on this one, Daisy, your mint julep is on me.

Regulations,
Dress

There's a big difference between style and fashion.

Dear Jimmy,
  I don't know if fashion is your topic of choice, but I like your common sense with other things, so maybe you'll answer this question. I dress up in a sport coat and tie every day for work. I like to dress up. On my casual days, I still dress in a shirt and tie, but I don't like to wear a sport coat. I would prefer my brown leather jacket. I only have two pairs of trousers that my brown shoes go with. Needless to say, I wear a lot of dark greys, blacks, and navy blues, so my shoe wardrobe is mostly black. My question is, would I get a fashion ticket if I wore my brown leather jacket with my black leather shoes?

—Ronnie, Ingraham, Pa.

I don't know anything about fashion. Look at my picture. I wear black and white. Period. But I think I've got style. "Style," at least to me, is when you dress in a way that makes you think you look good in what you're wearing no matter what you're wearing. Follow me?

So wear the brown jacket with the black shoes. Be confident and don't worry. If you have style, you'll pull it off fine. If you're a slave to fashion, you'll look like a putz. But it won't be because of your jacket-shoe combination.

Relationships,
Long-Distance

Distance makes the heart grow cold as ice.

Dear Jimmy,
   I'm a professional man in my mid-thirties. For the past year, I've been romantically involved with a woman who lives a long way away. We're doing the best that we can with this circumstance, but it's getting more difficult, not easier. Any suggestions for us? We're both deeply involved in our careers, so moving is out of the question.

—James, Chicago

If moving is out of the question because you're both deeply involved in your careers, then what's the point of this? Either do it as you have been doing it, or find somebody closer. Even if you figure out how to hardwire this long-distance romance, what will you get for your effort? You won't get much of a family, that's for sure. What you will get is a steady date with a woman you like. That description seems to me like it might fit more than one woman in the Chicago metropolitan area. So instead of running up phone bills and frequent-flyer miles, tell her goodbye and use that effort to find somebody in the neighborhood.

Relativity,
Theory of

Go ask Alice.

Dear Jimmy,

I think you're the kind of guy I can confide in. Here's the problem: I have a really small penis. I mean really small when it's *erect*. It's never bothered me before, but I'm only 21 years old and I've only had a couple of girls—and they were my friends, so they already knew about my size. It's getting to me now. I'm considering cosmetic surgery, even though I've heard it isn't safe. But I'm stuck with no other alternatives because I don't think I have the guts to bear women laughing at me. Do you have any advice?

—Rod, Guatemala City, Guatemala

Okay. You can confide in me. I won't tell a soul.

But you tell me why guys get so hung up on this. Too bad you don't live in America. You could park in handicapped spaces, and if anybody asked why, you could just point to your willie and say, "Very small."

Rod, there are two things men worry about: how much they make and how big they are. The average length of the average guy is exactly the same as the length of one Yankee dollar—about 6 inches. That's *average*. That means half the guys walking the planet have pocket change between their legs, and the other half have shorts full of Yahoo! stock. But here's the secret: Money won't make you a man. Neither will size. Whether it's your meat or your money, what matters is what you do with it.

Besides, you don't need me to tell you what you already know. You made it with a couple of women who were "friends." Your size didn't matter to you and it didn't matter to them. My advice is to make love only to women you love and women who love you. Then you won't have to worry.

Say,
What to, to a Woman

First things first. Then comes everything else. Or nothing at all.

Dear Jimmy,

I'm a somewhat successful, reasonably attractive guy, with one major problem: I don't know how to go up to a woman and start talking to her. What should I say to a woman so she'll like me?

—Dawson, Philadelphia

I've heard thousands of pickup lines from this side of the bar, and in all these years, I've heard only one that actually works: "Hi." I called a bunch of friends at different bars around the country and asked them what they've heard that works. There's a list of them on page 106. But let me tell you a secret. The first thing you say to a woman—whether it's "hello" or "God, I hate being rich and lonely"—isn't nearly as important as the second thing you say. If the second thing you say gets her to open up, you're home free.

So here's my advice: Introduce yourself. Then, for the second thing you say, ask her something about herself. Then—and this is important—shut up and listen. I've seen countless guys end up alone because they think impressing a woman means spelling out their life stories and sneering a bunch of double entendres. Salesmen call this a "shotgun" approach: Tell her everything, and maybe she'll find something to like.

Trust me, this strategy stinks. Instead of talking about you, talk about her, and once she's talking, don't interrupt. All a woman wants to know is if you're a man who pays attention to what really counts. And that's her.

Jimmy's List

Bar Commandments

Break any of these more than once, and you're condemned.

1. Thou shalt not whistle, yell, or bang on the bar to get the bartender's attention.

2. Thou shalt not ask the bartender to set up your sex life.

3. Thou shalt not spend 10 minutes figuring out who owes what on a 10-dollar bar tab.

4. Tip thy bartender as thyself.

5. Thou shalt not speak directly to a lady's cleavage without first obtaining the permission of the owner of the breasts.

6. Thou shalt not touch, pinch, fondle, or annoy the serving staff. This includes waitresses and barmaids.

7. Thou shalt not make any carven images on the bar surface or on the tops of the tables.

8. Thou shalt not sit on thy lunch, puke on thy shoes, or in any other way make the bartender responsible for your personal hygiene or the consequences of your environmental spills.

9. Thou shalt not smite thy drinking companion.

10. Thou shalt drink up at closing time.

Shadows,
Five O'Clock

Smooth beats suave every time.

Dear Jimmy,
   This is off your subject, but my wife is saying I look like a guy who doesn't know how to shave. I'm 40, for crying out loud. So what do you know about shaving that I don't?

—Daryl, Salt Lake City

This is a nutty question to ask a bartender, Daryl. You went through the Yellow Pages and none of the barbers answered their phones? I don't have any great secrets.

   Here's what I do. First off, I take a hot shower, as hot as I can stand it, and while still in the shower with the water running, I break out my razor. I use a single-blade mechanical job. I've had it since 1963. I use a new blade every 2 days, and I skip the shaving cream. I shave in the direction my beard grows, starting with my cheeks, then my moustache, then my chin and neck. Then I feel around for spots I missed. It must work because not a day goes by when some drunk broad doesn't lean over the bar to give your baby-faced Jimmy a little peck on the cheek, usually for being straight enough to tell her to go home.

Sin,
the Nature of

If it's bad for you, it always looks better than it is.

Dear Jimmy,
My girlfriend fakes an orgasm and then tells me she did. Is this the greatest compliment or a cardinal sin? I'm thinking of breaking up with her. What's your take?

—Todd, Toledo, Ohio

If it's a compliment, then you have a huge problem. If it's a cardinal sin, then she has a problem. The truth is, it's neither. Break up with her. She's too immature to handle a sex life, and if you have to ask this question, you are, too.

I used to have this woman who would always show up after work on Mondays. She was good-looking, funny, and bright, but she needed lots of attention. Most of the time, that was no problem. But during football season, she would fume. Why? Because she had to compete with the game. One night, she turns to me and asks me why men scream when their team makes a touchdown, but not when they're having sex. I told her what I'm telling you: Most men know the difference between scoring and making love. If all either of you is looking for is a score, then what the hell, a fake scream is just as loud as a real one. They both sound great in stereo. But if what you're looking to do is make love, then trust me. It's not the volume. It's the balance.

Sisters,
Dating Both

Blood is thicker than any guy's noggin.

Dear Jimmy,
  During a 3-year relationship with a woman, I flirted with her sister quite a bit. I recently broke up with the woman. Even though it wasn't friendly, I still talk to her sister. In fact, we're strongly attracted to each other. Do I pursue it?

—Ed, Miami

Jealousy between women is like a dog whistle; it can't be detected by men. I guarantee you that flirting with the sister had something to do with breaking up your romance. It bothers me when I see women doing that backstabbing routine with each other, because it always leaves the guy to pay the check. On the one hand, if you take up with sis, your ex is going to see it as revenge. You don't want that because, first, you don't want her to think you care that much, and second, you don't want to have a family feud as part of your romantic back-drop. On the other hand, if you walk away from both of them, your life is yours again. I say walk.

Take passion wherever you find it.

Dear Jimmy,
  I'm a big Orioles fan. I follow them from the first day of spring training until the next first day of spring training. But when they lose (and they usually lose), I get really upset, much more than I feel like I should. I mean, it's just a game, right? But it really depresses me. I guess this is a stupid question, but I could use some advice.

                                —Dix, Cumberland, Md.

I used to be a Birds fan. I know how you feel. But you asked yourself the right question. So answer it. Is it just a game? Well, yeah. But watching a game with your old man and rooting for your home team makes the whole thing about a lot more than just nine innings of mild suspense. It's about connecting with family or friends or the guys at work. And it's about loyalty, too, which in my eyes there ain't enough of these days. I got no problem with sports fans, as long as they don't spill their drinks or get too loud.

On the other had, if there's a lot of turmoil elsewhere in your life, then your worries aren't about a baseball team. Your problem is something else, and you have your wires crossed. Check around a little. Did you lose your job? Your wife leave you? Find what the problem is, because believe me, it isn't the Orioles. Just be glad you aren't a Cubs fan.

Stamina,
in the Bedroom

Stick-to-itiveness is what made America great.

Dear Jimmy,
  How can I make sex last longer?

—Frank, Laguna Niguel, Calif.

Depends. Longer than what? Longer than a baseball season? Longer than a Streisand movie? Longer than last time? I used to have the greatest customer. A doctor named—it's true—Welby. The guy was a butt man. Knew all about what made you do what you do from the waist down. It was great having him around because he'd field all these kinds of wise-guy questions.

Not that I ever needed this advice, but, uh, I do remember once when some kid did and asked Welby pretty much the same question you ask. I remember Welby said to masturbate an hour or two before the encounter, since that would take some of the edge off and help you concentrate on pleasing her, rather then taking care of number one.

He also used to advocate a kind of red-light/green-light routine, where you'd go right to the brink then the red light: stop. That usually got the lady's attention. Then green light, you're off again. He used to claim that if you paced yourself, you could go on like that for hours. Used to wear me out just listening to him rattle on about it.

Stepmothers,
Providing Support to

If it has a bull's-eye on it, somebody will throw a dart at it.

Dear Jimmy,

I've enjoyed your comments very much and would like to know if you have anything to say about this. I was married for 18 years and have two teenage boys. The ex took off to do new-age healing with rocks and smells, so I remarried.

Now I find myself living my life as a referee between my new wife and my sons. Most of the time, they get along great and we all have fun together. But my wife complains whenever she says something to the boys and I go against her. And the boys do the same if I take her side. It seems like I have to make all the final calls. How should I handle this?

—Randy, San Francisco

You have two grown-ups in your house, so pay attention to the other one. After all, it took guts to marry you with those two kids running around. Your new wife is their stepmother. But every time you reverse something she says or does or let the kids talk you into overruling her, you're telling them, "Well, this is just some dame I married, not your mother, so you can ignore her if you feel like it." Stop doing that. Sit the boys down, put your arm around your wife, and announce that there's no more running to you for a final verdict. You and she will make the decisions together until they become congressmen, make their own rules, and move out. What she says goes. What you say goes. And those two must always be the same, down to the word.

Stout,
How to Pour

First, add a dash of patience.

Dear Jimmy,
  I kind of like Guinness and those other stout ales, but I can't pour it right. I end up with a head the size of Rushmore. What's the secret?

—Lawrence, Superior, Nebr.

Depends. If you're drawing a proper pint—a 20-ounce Irish-size jar—hold the glass at about a 45-degree angle and let the stout hit the glass about two-thirds of the way up the side. Pull the tap handle toward you slowly until it's flat-out. Then, slowly bring the glass to vertical as it fills. When you've got it about three-quarters full, close the tap and set the glass aside for a minute while the head separates and floats to the top. Now, take the glass, hold it under the tap, and push the tap away from you for a second. This'll top it off right. The head should rise just above the glass's edge and shouldn't be more than three-quarters of an inch thick. If you're feeling fancy, trickle a crossed figure-eight on the head. If you don't quite finish the final eight, it'll look like a shamrock to a drunk.

Now, if it's a bottle of stout, you're working with something different. Guinness, not so much, but many fine stout ales have a good deal of sediment in the bottom of the bottle. Make sure the bottle has been kept still. Open it gently and pour on the 45, just like I described above. But this time, put your thumb under the spot where the beer hits the glass so the beer hits a warm spot. Take it slow and easy, and you'll get the whole bottle poured without a fuss. Stop when the sediment reaches the lip.

I serve stout at around 45 degrees Fahrenheit, but some bars serve it a little colder. Personally, I prefer it at almost room temperature. Same with porter.

Tab,
Picking Up the

If you're in the wrong, every round is your round.

Dear Jimmy,
   I've been dating my fiancée now for a little over 2 years. I know that I am in love with her and I never thought I could hurt her—until recently, when I switched jobs. Once a week, my buddies and I go out drinking, and one of them introduced me to a friend of his, a good-looking woman. Now, whenever we go out and I get quite a few beers in me, she and I can't seem to keep our hands off each other. Even though I haven't slept with her, I still feel that I need to tell my fiancée the truth. How can I pull this off without killing our relationship?

—John, Portsmouth, N.H.

Three little words nobody wants to hear from a bartender: "You've had enough." In other words, no more of this for you because you have to choose: The bim in the bar? Or the girl with the ring? Choose.

If you choose your drinkin' squeeze, then be honest with the girl whose heart you're going to break. Say this: "I was wrong. I'm not ready to get married." Then walk away.

If you choose your so-called fiancée, then tell the girl in the bar that you're engaged and you're serious about it.

But the one thing you can't tell the fiancée is what you've been doing behind her back. Just keep your mouth shut. You want to unload your guilt and convert it into somebody else's misery. Sorry, buddy. You ran up the bill. Pay it yourself.

Technology,
the Perils of

I remember the good old days, when a guy actually had to brush his teeth before he went out to pick up women.

Dear Jimmy,

I'm a 38-year-old male and have been married to the same woman for 18 years. I believe she loves me and I do love her. The problem is that she works at home on a computer all day, and in the process, she chats with men all day, every day, online. I suspect that she has personal conversations with men, and I know she has even called them on the phone. Should I ignore this situation and hope nothing happens, or confront her about it? I have mentioned it to her before, but she doesn't admit that anything fishy is going on.

—Paul, Phoenix

Something fishy's going on. I don't need the details. I've worked around this my whole life, so I can practically fill in the blanks for you. It used to be that when a woman wanted to meet a man, or when a man wanted to meet a woman, they'd both get decked out in their best and wander by a lounge, get tipsy enough to be indiscriminate, and see what happened next.

Now, instead of downtown barrooms, we have online chat rooms. Same thing, except everybody gets to show up in their underwear. This speeds everything up considerably. But the principle is the same: When a woman meets a guy in a bar or in a chat room, she doesn't know the guy from Adam. He's a clean slate on which she gets to project everything a man should be. In fact, because you don't have the obvious evidence of your eyes to get in the way, people look much better in a chat room than they do in a barroom. Everything gets speeded up. It's like super dog years; 1 hour in serious online chat with somebody is equal to a year of awkward dating.

Men and women both make a mess of all this. Over the years, I've seen a lot of romances that started in a bar and went outside to real life, where they usually fell apart. But there are far more of these online romances, and unless she's hormonally dead, chances are that she's at least flirting around the edges of one.

Here's a small consolation, though. As a rule, people look worse in real life than they do in people's fantasies. It's like meeting the world's ugliest woman in a bar, then waking up sober next to her in the morning. You think, "Damn! She looked great last time I saw her." So think of what she's doing as somebody who's spending all her time sitting in a singles bar, because that's exactly what a wired PC is like. Then give her whatever words of advice you think she needs to hear.

Jimmy's List

Regional Pick-Up Lines

I called up a bunch of bartenders and asked them for the best pick-up lines they've heard in the past year or so. And I gotta tell ya, this great country of ours is on the brink of collapse. In America, the land that practically invented inventiveness, these are the *best* we can do. Makes me want to cry.

Salt Lake City: Port o' Call—Erica
Guy says, "What screws like a tiger and winks?" Girl shakes her head—and the guy winks at her.

San Francisco: Gold Coast—Jason Skelly
Knock knock!
Who's there?
Emerson.
Emerson who?
Emerson nice hooters you have there.

San Francisco: Kate O'Brien's—Shannon
Show us the front of your bum.
This is more than a lousy pick-up line. It's also an Irish anatomy class.

Iowa City, Iowa: The Airliner—TJ
Are your legs tired? They should be because you've been running around in my mind all night.

Boston: Black Rose—Keith Doyle
That's a lovely dress you have on. Mind if I try to talk you out of it?

Baltimore: Club Charles—Mike
You look a lot like Veronica Lake. Mind if I take a swim?

Baltimore: Bohagers—Stephen Greul
If I could change the alphabet, I'd put "U" and "I" together.

(continued)

And this one: You may not like me now, but I'm drinking milk.

New Orleans: O'Flaherty's Irish Channel Pub—Terry Folan

Would you like to be buried with my people?
You have to be Irish to understand the charm of this one.

Portsmouth, NH: Bananas Bar and Grill—Albie MacDonald

Do you wash your clothes in Windex? Because I can see myself in your pants.

Miami: Corbetts Sports Bar and Grill—Margaret

I lost my phone number. Can I have yours?

Kansas City: North Side Lounge—Jerry

I had a dream about you last night.

Minneapolis: America Live—Kevin Blair

May I borrow 35 cents? My mother told me to call her when I fell in love.

Minneapolis: Sharx Club—John

What do you like for breakfast?

Seattle: Hop Vine Club—Amy

Are you from Tennessee? 'Cause you're the only "10" I see.

Chicago: Gilhooley's Grand Saloon—Kristin Rea

Man says, "Do you want to go to my place for pizza and sex?"
Woman says, "No!"
Man says, "What? You don't like pizza?"

Denver: Fado Irish Pub—Frank

Quit the grinnin' and drop the linen!

Denver: Legends—Alida

Don't I know you from somewhere?

Those are the best, mind you. No wonder we're limping into the next millennium: The whole nation has gone completely lame. One other thing: I have served approximately one billion drinks to women bought by some suave dude at the end of the bar. The success rate: About one in a billion. I have also served a grand total of one grilled cheese sandwich to a woman from a guy at the end of the bar. Success rate: 100 percent. Moral: Skip the shooter and stick with the cheese.

Teenage Girls,
Fathers of

Excuse me, your barn door's open.

Dear Jimmy,
  My daughter is 15 and she's starting to date. I can't stand the thought of those hormonal monstrosities she brings home putting their hands on her. What can I do to make sure she behaves herself?

—Swede, Des Moines, Iowa

She's 15? And now you're worrying about how she behaves? Reminds me of a gal who used to drink in my old place all the time. Good-looking woman, smart, but a nut case. She'd come in, get almost tipsy, then exaggerate it—slur her speech, laugh real loud, all of it—and then disappear with some jerk. It was like she needed an excuse to do something stupid. So one night, she comes in and the place is empty. So we get to talking. She sort of apologizes—to *me*, no less—for how she's been behaving. I said to her, "Well, I'm not your father, so I can't tell you what to do." She says, "My father didn't tell me what to do, either. Maybe that's my problem."

  The point is, if you're just now getting around to worrying about how the girl's going to behave on a date, you're way late to the party, pal. You've already had your chance to show her how to deal with this stuff. Now all you can do is be there for her if she makes one of the mistakes you taught her to make. Good luck, Pop. If I see her, I'll send her home.

Teenagers,
Grown Men Masquerading As

There's such a thing as a shaggy-dog question.

Dear Jimmy,

Here is my dilemma. I have been married for almost 2 years and have a wonderful, beautiful wife. We are expecting our first child next month. One thing I promised myself when I got married was that I would not stray from her. I cheated on her many, many times the first couple of years after we met. But I promised myself and my dead grandmother that I would never stray once I put the ring on her finger. And to be honest with you, it hasn't been that hard. When I go to the bars with my buddies, I see tons of gorgeous women with fabulous bodies and although I give a second look, I do not feel anything toward them in the least bit. I find these women very attractive, but those days are over, and my wife gives me 100 times more than the bar bombshells can.

However, I am attracted to my wife's best friend. She was the maid of honor in our wedding. She is also married (6 years) and has a 2-year-old boy. The thing is, she is not gorgeous and does not have a Baywatch body. She is just "Plain Jane." She's really nothing special, but I find myself definitely attracted to her. I don't want to screw up with my wife, and I don't want to mess things up with her marriage, either. I respect her and her family. I just think I want to enjoy a sexual experience with her before it's too late. Should I just see what happens? Please advise.

—Mike, Buffalo

I let guys like you ramble on like this for a reason. Sometime along about the third drink, the truth comes out, just like it did with you. You want to do all this "before it's too late."

Party's over, kid. You're a father now, so to at least one other person on the planet, you're what a man's supposed to be. No, don't screw your wife's best friend. Don't make a pass at her, even. If you're having a tough time making the switch-over from post-adolescence to adulthood, take the rough spots into the bathroom with you, lock the door, and don't come out until the pressure's off. You're like these teenage boys who come in here wearing their ball caps backwards and their trousers down below their butts and then try to pass me their fake IDs. I say to them the same thing I say to you, Mike: What the hell are you thinking?

Tipping,
the Science of

Fifteen percent of this, fifteen percent of that. It all adds up.

Dear Jimmy,
I am at a loss when it comes to tipping. I can figure out fifteen percent of a restaurant check, but what about all the other stuff? What about carpet installers? How about locksmiths? Valet parking—how much should I tip a valet? Should I tip when I give him the keys or when I get the car?

—Trey, Tucson

I depend on tips for my living, but there's one thing I can't stand: a guy who thinks his tip is going to make or break me. I'm a pro at what I do. If you like the service I give, fine. Tip me. If you don't, then tell me and don't tip me. But don't hold it over my head, because I won't bother to duck.

I'm getting that off my chest so you'll have a better idea of what a tip means to the people who count on them for their livelihood. That includes the boys who park your car. It doesn't include the guys who lay your carpet.

The rule for all tips is the same: Make it make sense. It doesn't make sense to give a guy a twenty for running for your car (and yes, you tip him when you're ready to leave). Figure it out. If he has to go twenty yards, give him a couple of bucks. If it's around the block, make it five. If it's raining, double everything.

For all those other tips of the locksmith variety, make a tip a reward for something extraordinary, not for just showing up to do a job. If the locksmith is letting you into your apartment, pay the bill and say, "See ya." If he's letting you into Yasmine Bleeth's apartment, slip him an extra fiver.

Wages,
Determining Fairness of

What's a human life worth? Don't ask your boss.

Dear Jimmy,
I have a good job and I'm slowly moving up the ladder. But my company has a history of bringing in new hires at a higher pay rate than what they are giving existing employees. When this happened to me a year ago, it was solved with a raise fairly fast. Now I've learned that they've done it again. Upper management says they value me as an employee, but I don't want to be taken advantage of anymore. Should I look for new challenges?

—Gary, Mobile, Ala.

Sounds like you have a challenge right where you are. It's tricky, I admit. I'm a guy who hasn't asked for a raise ever. Instead, when I want to do better, I do better for my customers. My tips go up and I'm happy. It's a little different for you because what you're worth to your boss doesn't have anything to do with what they're paying somebody else. Your worth is determined by only two things: First, by how much your boss is paying you to do your job. You already have the answer to that. Second, what somebody else is willing to pay you to do the same job. You'll have to find the answer to that one.

So if you want more money, do these things in this order: First, make sure that you're doing the best work you can do. Second, start making friends with the competition. Just drop a word here and there. Wait until you get some interest from one of them. Third, get a firm offer. Fourth, sit down with your boss and tell him that you think equal pay for equal work is a pretty good concept. If he disagrees, accept the competition's offer. If he agrees, listen to his offer. The highest offer is the amount you're worth to an employer.

Warrior,
Weekend

All right, men. Move out! But take her with you.

Dear Jimmy,
My wife and I have been happily married for 10 years now. All is good with the family and the job. But our love life has gone by the wayside since the birth of our two children. Any suggestions for help to get the fire back in the relationship? I'm talking about a quick-fix remedy. Thanks for your ear.

—T. J., Pittsburgh

The Army Reserves has a plan for you. Pack up your wife, leave the kids with your sister-in-law, and get out of town together one weekend every month. Leave the house and don't bring the kids; the only toys and dirty clothes on the hotel floor should be yours. Eat a nice meal. Make each other laugh. Once you have a few of these mini-elopements under your belt, and you both know another one is coming soon, it'll help fuel sex at home, too. Trust Jimmy. Now quit talking to me, get out your map, and head for the horizon.

Wines,
How to Pick

What are you? Something fruity?

Dear Jimmy,
Which wines do you drink with which dishes?

—Bob, Novato, Calif.

As a bartender, I don't care what wine anybody drinks. I'll serve whatever they ask for. As a guy who likes an occasional glass of wine with supper, I'm pretty traditional. If it's a steak or some spicy pasta dish, I like to order a good French Bordeaux—I'm kind of crazy about the ones from right around Pauillac. I think the stuff tastes good with most red meats. My rule, though, is that if the serving of meat is less than 4 ounces, you can give me a brew. Also, I hate spending more than 25 or 30 bucks for a bottle of wine. I can find plenty that are good enough to drink for under 20, including a lot of merlots. With a hearty fish dish, like salmon, I'll take a glass of California pinot noir. With everything else—shrimp or veggie dishes or what have you—just give me whatever's coldest, driest, and whitest.

Now that I've spouted off like some kind of wine snob, let me also tell you, Bob, that it's a mistake to grow an insecurity about wine or any other up-market preoccupation. Take cigars. You keep your Cohibas. Give me an Amish butt. It has a Pennsylvania wrapper and fill, it's handmade by all those barn-raisers, and it stinks up the house as well as any Cuban import. Costs two bucks. Same with wine. Order what you like.

The thing with all these kinds of trendy things is there are a lot of insecure people around hoping you don't know what you're doing so they can look like they do. So if you simply look like you know what you're doing, they'll feel like they don't. And they'll be right.

Wives,
Ex-, Wanting to Reunite with

Go back to the future without any special effects.

Dear Jimmy,
My wife and I divorced about 3 years ago. It was my fault. Even though we had three great kids, the marriage wasn't going so well, so I started fooling around and got caught. I've been having a great time, but now I've met a new woman, and this time I think it's the right one. So now my ex throws me for a loop. She says she's willing to get back together again. She says it will be better for the kids. I see them almost every day as it is, and they are kind of unhappy about how the situation stands now. But this new woman in my life is everything I ever wanted. She's married now, but they're getting a divorce soon. Any ideas?

Burt, Denver

Well, at least you're asking. I have to say that I admire a guy who wants to order another but isn't sure he should. So he'll say, "Jimmy, think I should have another?" I almost always say, "If you have to ask, the answer's no."

In your case, the answer's yes, but to your wife. So far, going for everything you ever wanted has cost you the happiness of your family, the people who counted on you to always do the right thing. So now, to make yourself feel better, you're going to help screw up another family. When the dust settles from all of this, you think you're going to be happy? Only if your soul dies, buddy. Your wife is giving you a chance to undo a huge mistake. Take her up on it. You may think that you're going to be giving up your shot at happiness, but take it from me. You can't get happy by being selfish. Your wife's giving you the last chance at happiness you're going to get in this life. You owe her big time. Good luck.

Wives,
Neglect of

The good news and the bad news: You're not suffering alone.

Dear Jimmy,

How do you forget the woman you love, especially when you have no right to be in love with her? I have been married for 19 years to a woman that I like very much—but I do not love her. I have known this since the night we were married. I have two lovely daughters and I share much in their lives. But I do not share anything with their mother; we are complete opposites. It's funny, but in the 20 years I have known her, she has never really said anything to me. I try to talk to her about her feelings and opinions, but she gets mad and says it's too personal. I even tried a counselor, but she refused to talk to the man.

The problem is that I found the woman I love about 7 years ago. I met her in Myrtle Beach. You could say it was just one of those summer things, but it was more, and we both knew it from the start. I told her I was married and that I could not leave my children without them understanding why. We saw each other for 7 years. I always told her that I could not hold her back from doing what she wanted, but it didn't seem to matter to her. Finally, last year, I decided that my children were old enough to understand, so I went to her and asked her if she still wanted me. She said she did. Our relationship became very intense, and to tell you the truth, it even scared me a little, even though I loved her.

But then things went wrong. She wanted me to move away from my family. I told her that I had no problem with that but that I had to buy another place, which I did. While this was going on, another man became involved with her. She told me about him. I told her that I would not forbid her from talking to him, that they were friends and friends are special and should never be tossed out. She started to become cold and mean. I went down to Miami to see her. She tried to make things as tough as possible. It was almost as if she tried to make me hate her. Well, things did not work out too well and I left early. I told her that I wished her the best and that I will always love her, but I would not stand in the way of her happiness.

Well, it's been a year now and I find that I still miss her. In my heart, I know that she was truly that rare thing—I think they call it your soul mate. So here I am, still with my wife who I like, but with my heart belonging to a woman I love. I let her go so she could be happy, but life is just not the same. Do you understand?

—Chris, Baltimore

Sure. But if you think you have it rough, you should see the woman who married you.

Women,
Blindness of

When it comes to men, some women are like a blind man in an art gallery: He doesn't know what he sees, but he knows what he wants to see.

Dear Jimmy,

I've fallen for this woman like a nearsighted roofer. Unfortunately, she's engaged, but her unscrupulous fiancé is hitting on my secretary. My heart is killing me. How can I let her marry him? What should I do?

—Jack, Indianapolis

I get these guys who drink a lot and then want to fight, but they can't manage it because they can't find anybody to fight with. Don't be like them. Make the guy an enemy. Talk to him. Tell him he's a jerk and that if he were a man, he'd break up with her. He'll tell you to get lost. You tell him he's a son of a bitch. He'll despise you; you'll despise him. That's war. All's fair in war, including love. Which is how you'll be able to bring yourself to tell her that he's been hitting on your secretary.

Women,
Friends Who Are, Part One

Just remember to keep your nose out of their business.

Dear Jimmy,
  I have a friend who is a girl. She's 22. I'm 25. Of all the friends I have, she's the one that I love hanging out with. I have a problem though: Sometimes, when we've been out having a good time, we end up getting sexually involved. Then we end up trying to turn our friendship into a romantic relationship, because that is what she wants. But I am not really attracted to her in that way. So I want to know how I can end our sexual relationship once and for all and still maintain her friendship, which I value so much?

—Ron, Urbana, Ill.

Frankly, you have nobody to blame for this but yourself. I used to have a customer like you. It was a woman, sweetest thing you'd ever want to meet. Guys would fall over themselves for her. But she made more enemies than anybody I ever met. How? By not playing it straight with them.

You're doing the same thing with this girl. You're being her friend, you're doing everything right, saying all the right things, doing all the right moves, except for one thing. You sleep with her. So the answer's pretty simple. If you want to be her friend, treat her like a friend, not like a lover. That means no sneaking between her legs just because you're out having fun. Don't let her have any hope that your friendship can be more than just that. If you play it straight, she's your friend. If you give her even one mixed signal, she's your lover now and your enemy later.

Women,
Friends Who Are, Part Two

Believe it or not, if the question's big enough, it doesn't matter what the answer is.

Dear Jimmy,
   I have a query and I was hoping you might be able to give me some advice. You've heard this one a thousand times, I'm sure, but there is this girl that I think is absolutely incredible. She is truly one in a million. I could live a million years and never find another like her, and I am head-over-heels crazy about her. The problem is, she doesn't see me the same way. I don't want to ruin a great friendship, but I'm driving myself nuts thinking about her. Should I tell her? Or bottle it up and deal with it? Take care, and thank you.

—Daniel, Cincinnati

Deal with it, but skip the bottle. The fact is, she already knows exactly how you feel about her, and she's made it pretty clear how she feels about you. Now, if you want to continue this friendship or whatever you call it, be my guest. But don't think it'll ever be any more than that. You can't make women feel something they don't feel. The only way you're ever going to make this girl feel something toward you is to never ask her to feel anything other than what she feels right now.

Women,
Ladies' Room Habits of

The miracles of migration: You got your farmers moving west, your geese flying south, your killer bees moving north, and your women going to the john.

Dear Jimmy,
   Why do women go to the bathroom in groups?

—John, Syracuse, N.Y.

Saloons are full of Nature's mysteries. Why do smart guys drink until they're stupid? Why do waitresses improve in appearance between midnight and 2:00 A.M.? Why is the amount of the tip in inverse proportion to the loudness of the tipper?

I worked at a place in Flushing for about 10 minutes one time. Awful bar, but it had this little slip of paper on the wall by the phone. It listed 10 reasons why women go to the bathroom in groups. I don't remember it all, but it went something like this: because the wind blows from the west; because the sun rises in the east; because hot air rises; because cold air sinks.

And so on, until it got to number 10, which was: because they all have to take a leak.

Personally, I think it's number 10. The fact that they gossip about their dates, share makeup, talk about sex, borrow tampons, fix wedgies, and scope out other men in the bar on the way is purely coincidental. By the way, men's rooms are hygienic heavens compared to the hell of a ladies' room on a Saturday night. What *are* they doing in there?

Women,
Lying

This is a major category—almost as major as the
"Men, Lying and Cheating" category (see page 59).

Dear Jimmy,
   I've been dating this girl for about 2 months. She has one kid, and she told me she was divorced. But about 2 weeks ago, I found out that she was only separated. She says she loves me, but I have caught her in several lies. What should I do?

—Eric, Des Moines, Iowa

You already know what to do because it's what you wish you'd done when you first thought to ask me. What a mess. Lying about being married isn't like her lying about being 128 pounds or about hitchhiking across Nevada with Billy Carter back in 1978. It's a big, dangerous lie that hurts a bunch of people—you, that poor tyke who wonders why you're playing daddy, and the guy on her marriage license who's probably at your door right now. Get me? No? Well, look at it this way. In a tavern, when a fight breaks out and the bartender can't stop it within 10 seconds, it's out of control. If you're a smart guy, at that point, you'll ask your buddy if he's ready to go. If he says no, then you do the smart thing: You leave alone. Now I'm telling you, Eric, that woman's a barroom brawl. Beat it.

Women,
Meeting Online

What you see is what you get. What you read is wishful thinking.

Dear Jimmy,

There's a woman I've been talking to online for about a year now. She and I have grown very close. We're both married and both have kids. But we find that we give each other something that's missing in our marriages. Now we're thinking of meeting, and if it goes well, taking it from there. Before you call me crazy, we have probably spent more time talking in a year than most people do in a lifetime. We've exchanged photos, so we're certainly not strangers, and we're not kids either—I'm in my early fifties, she's 36.

—Bob, Chicago

No, I'm not going to call you crazy. In fact, I think you're the man of the future. You remind me of a guy who used to come in here all the time ordering those miserable bottled wine-and-seltzer concoctions. What do you call them? Wine coolers. He never liked the stuff, but every time they'd run a new television ad, he'd give it another shot, then gripe about it. So I asked him, "Why do you keep coming back for more?" He said, "I just know one day it's going to taste as good as it looks on the screen."

I don't know anything about this computer stuff. Maybe one day, everybody will tele-court and tele-wed, tele-parent and tele-commute. But until then, for the guys who haven't yet figured out how to meet women right away, I just want to say watch out for all these Internet chat rooms. You know how they say a camera adds 10 pounds to a woman's weight? Well, I'm going to guess that a chat room takes off about 125 pounds, minimum. So you have this electronic dating game whose main participants are giant women and 15-year-old boys. Then there's you, Bob. I bet there are plenty of 40- and 50-year-old guys on the Internet, too, because it's the only place on Earth they can get pretty young women to talk to them.

You have a wife, as you might have noticed. She's the woman you wake up next to every day, the one who washes your soiled briefs. If you want your wife to be an ideal woman, get her onto the Internet, give her a screen name with "Julia" or "Jennifer" in it, and type dirty to her. But one thing's for sure: If you try to make your virtual reality real, you won't be in virtual trouble. You'll have a lap-load of the real thing.

Women,
Supply and Demand

Scarcity makes strange bedfellows.

Dear Jimmy,
   How do I meet a woman when I want to? Every relationship I've had just sort of happened without me looking. These days, though, I'm not having any luck meeting women, and I'm getting a little needy.

—Jim, Indianapolis

Meet Howard Feinman. Howie has been stalking me from bar to bar for more than 20 years. He's more than a regular by now. He's my favorite drinking buddy. Here's how I met him. I was working in Manhattan, and one rainy day, this big lug comes walking in out of the downpour. The guy looks like a bag of clothes. He orders, I pour, and he wrings himself out. I find out he's a cabbie. I say, "Hey, it's pouring rain out there. You've gotta be missing a lot of business." He says, "Nah, I'm done for the day. I just can't stand that much desperation."

   Women on good days are like cabs on bad ones. They know they've got what you want, and they hate your desperation. On the other hand, you can't just make up indifference. It comes off as arrogance. Put this kind of problem in front of a crowded bar, where the only good reasons for being there are to get stupid or get laid—there's a difference?—and you're going nowhere faster than Howie in the rain. Try someplace else, someplace where you have something else to do other than scoring babes. In other words, meet a woman when you're busy with your life. Gyms are good, and so are supermarkets, bookstores, and bike paths. I hear that if you want to meet a soul mate, you should go to church. But I got that from my brother, who isn't even married. He's a priest.

Jimmy's List

Best Ballpark Brews

A buddy of mine, Limmy Lewis, worked for 10 years in the stands at Ebbett's Field in Brooklyn. He's dead now, like the Brooklyn Dodgers. Anyways, before he croaked, here's what Limmy told me about baseball and beer.

"The reason a baseball game has nine innings is because you need three innings to eat your franks, drink a beer, and buy the kids junk. Then you need two innings to drink another brew. Then you need an inning to find the men's room. Two more innings for another suds. The last inning is a safety idea: You need at least six outs after a beer before getting in a car."

Personally, I like beer and ball. It's a great combination, if you ask me. Here are the standings, in my book. I think you'll be hoping for extra innings if you're at a game in one of these parks.

1. AMERICAN LEAGUE EAST: CAMDEN YARDS. I used to love a beer called National Bohemian. Just asking for a National Bohemian made you feel a little heady. Maybe that's why the Baltimore locals called it "Boh," back when the Orioles were a great working-man's team. But Camden Yards is too upmarket for that, I guess. Michelob will have to get you through early innings, but after the stretch, grab a Pete's Summer Brew or a J. W. Dundee.

2. AMERICAN LEAGUE CENTRAL: METRODOME. Great beer, but the Minnesota Twins sure have a lousy ballpark. It's like watching nine innings in a giant elevator. Maybe that's why I like Grain Belt Premium. They also had a microbrew last time I was there—James Page's, I think it was.

(continued)

3. American League West: Edison Field. You can get Tecate there, with lime even. No wonder they all look like Angels in the outfield.

4. American League Wild Card: Jacobs Field. The Indians are a great club to watch. Plus, you can get some terrific regional brews. Here's a batting order: Crooked River, Elliot Ness, Cool Mule, and Pride of Cleveland—"POC" to the locals.

The senior circuit's got a few, too.

1. National League East: Veterans Stadium. Lots of good brews in Philadelphia, but not a lot of them make it onto the taps in the Phillies' ballpark. You'd think you were settling for Miller's, but truth is, it's a fine mass-produced lager, about right for mass-produced NL East baseball. On your way home, grab some Yuengling lager. I love that stuff.

2. National League Central: Wrigley Field. Since it's the Chicago Cubs playing out there, you'd think they'd serve 100-proof beer in the stands. But the preferred brew, Old Style, is a winner, and Goose Island, the boutique choice, is a game beer, too. So, unlike the home team, you can't lose.

3. National League West: Coors Field. Hey. It's in Colorado. It's called Coors Field. Guess what the Rockies' home brew is? There's a joint called Sand Lot Brewery in the park. Nice place for a cold one. Altitude helps.

4. National League Wild Card: Milwaukee County Stadium.
The Brewers used to be an American League franchise. Then they started selling Sprecher's beer, and they outclassed the league. The guy who used to supervise Pabst's brewery makes this stuff out in Glendale, Wisconsin, and it's the best ballpark brew in America. I personally think the Brewers are a boring ball team, but I'd buy a season box and go to every game just for a chance to soak up a Sprecher's or two or three. These guys even make a great grown-up root beer.

Women,
Understanding the Meaning of

You can read between the lines all you want, but sometimes, there's just nothing there.

Dear Jimmy,
From the time I left college, I kept getting involved with women who thought I was attractive to start with, then after 6 months or a year would decide to break up with me. They could never give me a good reason why; they would usually blame themselves or give some lame excuse like we weren't right for each other or that we would be better off just as friends. I went through this four times in my twenties. Now I'm almost 30, and it's happening to me again. I should be able to learn something from this, but it just doesn't make any sense to me. I try to be nice and patient and understanding, but it always leads to the same place. So let me ask you: What the hell do women *really* mean when they say, "It's not you, it's me"?

—Jared, Freehold, N.J.

They mean it's you.

When a woman wants to stop seeing you because of some reason that makes her feel bad about herself—if, for example, she thinks you're "too nice"—then she'll say that the reason she doesn't want to see you anymore is because she's "bad" and you're "good." But the real reason is that you tried too hard or something like that. "Nice" and "patient" and "understanding" are great attributes for nurses, elderly bartenders, and grandfathers. If you're none of these, then maybe you should go for something closer to "assertive" and "driven" and "judgmental," because those are things she won't tolerate in any man, except the man she loves.

Women,
Use of the Word *Fat* around

Not in the dictionary. Sorry.

Dear Jimmy,
  I've been dating my girlfriend for about 2 years, and in the past 6 months, she's put on about 20 pounds. I've tried to get her to work out with me and be more active, but she always has some excuse. I want to tell her she's getting heavy, but all my buddies tell me it's a bad idea and that she has to figure it out for herself. If I say something, I'm sure it will make me look like a "bad," insensitive guy, but if I don't, well, I'm afraid she'll keep gaining weight. What can I say or do?

—Alex, San Diego

Alex, you're officially the millionth guy to ask me this question. My answer is always the same. If you have a rock-hard stomach yourself, and you don't mind going without sex for 6 months, by all means, tell her she's getting fat. I know, I know. You're thinking, "Well, not in those words." But it doesn't matter how you say it, because if "you're getting fat" is what you mean, then "you're getting fat" is what she'll hear.

You have two alternatives. One is to start working out yourself and ask her if she'd keep you company. The other is to keep quiet. Believe me, she knows she's carrying the extra tonnage, and she doesn't need you pointing it out.

Since you're my millionth, I'll add a bonus tip. Alex, maybe tomorrow, maybe in 10 or 20 years, she's going to go full-porker. There's no stopping it. That's what some women do. That's all right. You might go bald. If you wouldn't make love to her plump, and she wouldn't screw you bald, you two are only temporary anyway. In that case, have fun until one of you meets a real sweetheart.

Women,
Wounded

Sometimes, it's dangerous being safe.

Dear Jimmy,

I am a 26-year-old male and my problem, if that's what you want to call it, is that I seem to only attract older divorced women who have one kind of problem or another. What is it that I am doing wrong?

—Luis, Santa Barbara, Calif.

Depends on the woman, of course. In fact, everything *always* depends on the woman. Chances are, these walking wounded find you to be "safe." I'm thinking that these women regard you with the same wholesome fondness that toothless people regard mashed potatoes. Or, if the troubled women you're attracting want to work out revenge on you for all the wrongs that they've suffered, then make sure you're not volunteering to be what the science guys call a "masochist." If that's your taste, I can't help you much, son.

Look, here it is straight: If you don't want to settle down with an older divorcée, stop spending your social time being an ear to them. Go where single women go, and find something interesting to say to them. If you're not as successful, don't worry. In 10 years, you'll have more dinged-up honeys than you'll know what to do with.

Work,
Being Paid to

These aren't the Olympics. We're all being paid to do this.

Dear Jimmy,
I have the feeling I'm about to be fired. Do I work harder to try to save my job or just quit? Should I approach my boss with my suspicions? Should I just wait for the axe to fall to get severance?

—Mike, Dallas

What if I were asking you that question? Let's say you come in here and order a Gibson, and I say, "You know, Mike, I think the manager's gonna can me. So should I just tell you to make your own damn drink? Or should I make you the best Gibson you've ever had?" My point is, unless you're working as a hobby, always be a pro. Do the best job you can, even after you get your pink slip. Do this not because your boss will feel like a jerk for firing you. He won't. But if you go out giving it your best, you'll feel a lot better about yourself.

Also, my guess is that it'll shorten the time you spend looking for a new job by more than half. Why? You'll have some self-respect, and your old boss might even give you a hand.

Work,
Policing the Atmosphere at

Inside every office and factory is a little ozone layer. Below it, there are a bunch of people worrying about the stuff they can't see.

Dear Jimmy:

I work at a company with about two dozen employees. Two of my married co-workers have been having an affair for some time now. They have never admitted it, but they spend a lot of lunches together and happen to share some of the same random days off. I am hesitant to approach the guy (who has three kids) because I have to spend all day with him. If I confront him about this big mistake, how can I protect myself from creating a poor working environment?

—Sean, Green Bay, Wis.

I used to know a bartender—a little tiny guy named Hyman, if you can believe it—who was real proud of how much he knew about all of his customers. We shared a shift in this big, ritzy place, and all the people who came in had big bucks. Hy thought he knew them all. He'd gossip about their wives and their kids and the money they were making. When somebody wanted to know something, they'd always go to Hy. Me, I kept my mouth shut and poured drinks. He made a killing in tips. The guy had a tip cup that would fit Dolly Parton. Me, I'd be lucky to make half of what he brought down.

One day, a regular, a famous football player, a guy who had two Super Bowl rings and a whole damn entourage, comes in. This time, though, he's alone and he's looking real long, practically in tears. He walks up to the bar and Hy gives him the hiya-old-pal routine. The guy reaches across the bar and pulls Hy up over the counter, but carefully, so he doesn't break anything, including Hyman. The little guy looked like a pimiento, hanging there in mid-air, turning red. The football player brings him right up to his face and says, "You told a lie about me, and it got back to my kids. It hurt them. You ever mention my name again, I'll break you in two." Then he puts Hy back and walks out. Hy, he staggered around like a bad drunk, stammering about how he hadn't said anything. But word got around. Everybody knew he'd said something because he'd told them. Two months later, he was fired for telling a story about a TV writer who was a friend of the owner.

The thing is, both times, I thought he was telling the truth. And both times, he thought he was doing the right thing by telling it. The point here is that if you don't know what you're talking about, then don't talk. People ruin their lives all the time. Sometimes, they do it by screwing over their families. Sometimes, they do it by spreading lies.

Work,
Rules for Dating Women at

Women. You can work with 'em all day, or you can sleep with 'em all night. Take your pick, or look for other work.

Dear Jimmy,
I'm a fellow bartender. I work with a beautiful waitress and we're getting close. Should I ask her out? How do you feel about dating people you work with?

—Kyle, Lexington, Ky.

How do *I* feel? Well, there are no waitresses in my bar, and I have to tell you, I wouldn't go on a date with one of these regular mooks if they were begging to be taken out and shot. But I have worked in bars—excuse me, "cocktail lounges"—that had waitresses—excuse me, "servers"—and before I got married, I dated some and never had a problem. So what can you learn from that? Just this: Go ahead and date a woman you work with, just as long as where you work is a place where everybody sits around drinking too much and getting blind-stupid.

But let's assume you decide that pouring drinks isn't a growth industry and you want to trade your bow tie for a necktie. So you get a job in an office. Now, instead of being surrounded by people who are trying hard to misbehave and lose their inhibitions, you're working with people whose idea of a good time is exploring "process." Is it still safe to date the women you work with? Not on your life. I hear these office types yapping at happy hour every day, and let me tell you, an office is nothing but a battlefield. Sleep with a co-worker, and it will become a weapon against you, used first by your co-workers, then, someday, by your bed partner. Trust me here. Skip the cubicle cuties and date women who work in bars, instead.